Supporting Children of Incarcerated Parents in Schools

Drawing on qualitative research conducted with young people in New York City, this volume highlights the unique experiences of children of incarcerated parents (COIP) and counters deficit-based narratives to consider how young people's voices can inform and improve educational support services.

Supporting Children of Incarcerated Parents in Schools combines the author's original research and personal experiences with an analysis of existing scholarship to provide unique insight into how COIP experience schooling in the United States. With a focus on the benefits of qualitative research for providing a more nuanced portrayal of these children and their experiences, the text foregrounds youth voices and emphasizes the resilience, maturity, and compassion which these young people demonstrate. By calling attention to the challenges that COIP face in and out of school, and also addressing associated issues around race and racism, the book offers large- and small-scale changes that educators and other allies can use to better support children of incarcerated parents.

This volume will be of interest to scholars and researchers interested in the sociology of education, race and urban education, and the impacts of parental incarceration specifically. It will also be of benefit to educators and school leaders who are supporting young people affected by these issues.

Whitney Q. Hollins is an Adjunct Lecturer in Youth Studies at the CUNY School of Professional Studies and CUNY Hunter College, USA.

Routledge Research in Educational Equality and Diversity

Books in the series include:

Global Perspectives on Microaggressions in Schools
Understanding and Combating Covert Violence
Edited by Julie K. Corkett, Christine L. Cho and Astrid Steele

Working-Class Masculinities in Australian Higher Education
Policies, pathways, progress
Garth Stahl

Indigenous Identity Formation in Chilean Education
New Racism and Schooling Experiences of Mapuche Youth
Andrew Webb

Supporting Children of Incarcerated Parents in Schools
Foregrounding Youth Voices to Improve Educational Support
Whitney Q. Hollins

The Hidden Academic Curriculum and Inequality in Early Education
How Class, Race, Teacher Interactions, and
Friendship Influence Student Success
Karen Phelan Kozlowski

For more information about this series, please visit: www.routledge.
com/Routledge-Research-in-Educational-Equality-and-Diversity/
book-series/RREED

Supporting Children of Incarcerated Parents in Schools

Foregrounding Youth Voices to Improve Educational Support

Whitney Q. Hollins

Routledge
Taylor & Francis Group

NEW YORK AND LONDON

First published 2022
by Routledge
605 Third Avenue, New York, NY 10158

and by Routledge
2 Park Square, Milton Park, Abingdon, Oxon, OX14 4RN

Routledge is an imprint of the Taylor & Francis Group, an informa business

Library of Congress Cataloging-in-Publication Data
A catalog record for this title has been requested

ISBN: 978-1-032-06160-3 (hbk)
ISBN: 978-1-032-06414-7 (pbk)
ISBN: 978-1-003-20214-1 (ebk)

DOI: 10.4324/9781003202141

Typeset in Times New Roman
by codeMantra

This book is dedicated to the children of incarcerated parents, who often have so much to say and so few places to say them. This is your space.

Contents

Acknowledgments

First and foremost, I'd like to acknowledge that this book was written during the COVID-19 pandemic and while everyone has been affected by the virus, this has been a particularly trying time for incarcerated people and their families. America's jails and prisons provide little space for social distancing and people who are incarcerated were often the last to receive protective measures such as masks and vaccines, if they received them at all. In 2021, the *New York Times* declared that "America's prisons, jails and detention centers have been among the nation's most dangerous places when it comes to infections from the coronavirus" (p.1). This must be extremely frightening for anyone who is incarcerated, but is also stressful for their loved ones, including their children. Being the child of an incarcerated parent can already be traumatic, and when a virus is ravaging the country and your parent cannot protect themselves, it becomes even more so. Anecdotally, I have had heard stories of children who have been unable to physically visit their parent for over a year while simultaneously being afraid to talk to them on the phone because of the crowded conditions around the phones in jails and prisons and the risk this may pose. I have also heard discussions about permanently replacing in-person visiting with the virtual visiting that has been utilized in some institutions during the pandemic. Although this book doesn't have the scope to address the devastation that COVID-19 has caused for incarcerated people and their families, it is heavy on my mind. Even when the pandemic is over, the scars will remain and the fight for the rights of incarcerated people and their loved ones will continue.

I'd also like to acknowledge the researchers, advocates, and activists who have previously devoted their time and talent to supporting children of incarcerated parents. As the child of an incarcerated parent, it brings me joy to know so many people recognize the community and are working tirelessly to ensure we receive the support we need.

This book advocates for the use of qualitative research methods to explore the nuances and complexities about the lives of children of incarcerated parents, which I believe are too numerous to be captured by purely quantitative data. This is not meant to be a criticism of previous quantitative work which has provided invaluable insights and information, but instead, a way forward. I am aware that some people may find my approach too unscientific or biased. However, I would argue that the status quo Eurocentric research is often inherently biased and that there are multiple approaches to gathering data. Humans are prone to subjectivity and instead of trying to obscure mine, I hope to own it. However, the words of the youth in this book speak for themselves. They do not require my interpretation, even though sometimes I venture to give it. This book also forefronts race, or more specifically racism, which I believe is central to understanding mass incarceration and its collateral consequences. I hope that people who read this book will understand that not only did I conduct research on this topic, but that my life could also be considered research. I am offering an alternate way to view and approach many of the issues that affect children of incarcerated parents, not the ultimate way. My hope is that research in this area continues to grow and that my research will provide a useful tool for other people who want to support this population in the future.

In addition, I'd like to acknowledge the hard work that educators and teachers do every single day. Yes, even on Saturday and Sunday. As a former teacher, I know that a career in education can feel both rewarding and thankless. The pandemic has illustrated just how many amazing teachers there are all over this country. It is one of the nation's most important jobs. Nonetheless, there are things that need improvement. On an individual level, educators, myself included, could stand to be reflective about how our own experiences shape the ways we interact with our students. In a larger context, it is important to examine how whiteness informs our perceptions of schools and schooling and how this perpetuates systems of inequality. This is heavy work, but if we seek to maintain our commitment to all students, it is necessary. We cannot continue to espouse the virtues and values of education without a realistic look at how the promise of education means different things to different groups of children.

Lastly, I'd like to acknowledge my support system which happens to include many other children of incarcerated parents. My family –my son, mother, father, siblings, and grandparents – always encourages me to pursue my dreams, including authoring this book. As the child of a formerly incarcerated parent writing something that could help directly impacted children is a great honor. My friends often provide the support needed to work toward my goals, frequently acting as an informal babysitters club. The tremendous joy and stress that parenthood creates has underscored just how important my village is. I'd like to thank my dissertation committee who never questioned my vision and told me that my study was worth a book and numerous articles. They encouraged me to find my authentic voice within academia instead of trying to make me assimilate. Finally, the directly impacted community has provided me with lifelong mentors, colleagues, and friends. At times when I doubt myself, I am encouraged by their stories and optimism. They inspire me to keep pushing forward and speaking my truth, regardless of the status quo. I plan to make them proud.

In solidarity,

Whitney

Reference

The New York Times. (2021). Infected and incarcerated: How the virus tore through the U.S. prison system.

Introduction

A Personal Testimony of My Childhood Experience with Parental Incarceration

> People closest to the problem are closest to the solution, but furthest from power and resources.
>
> (Glenn E. Martin)

Whenever I visit my grandmother's house, I stop to view the treasure trove of family photographs. Our family is all there, mounted on the walls and resting on wood furniture. However, there are some pictures that are not quite like the rest. There's one in particular that always catches my attention for a number of reasons. This picture is somewhat of a rarity. It features my grandmother, my now deceased aunt, my father, and both of my brothers. My brothers and I are young. I am sitting with them on a wicker bench as the adults stand behind us. My hair is cut short, a decision that was made because I absolutely hated getting my hair done and loved the sophisticated looks of 1990s it girls Halle Berry and Toni Braxton. The fact that I did not like getting my hair done is evident in the picture as a sizable poof of hair sits on top of my head and the sides are clean shaven. I have on a quintessential 1990s outfit. My socks are pulled up high. I am wearing a patterned vest. I have on sneakers with chunky soles. The rest of my family's outfits reflect the time as well, perhaps with the exception of my grandmother. Her look has been consistent for as long as I can remember. My dad is sporting a long beard and jeans that look acid wash, but not quite. For most people, this picture may be a slightly embarrassing, but adorable family relic. For me, it's a mystery. A reminder of a time that I am aware existed, but I cannot quite recall in detail. I simply cannot remember when I first realized my father was in prison. For the most part, it feels like that's where he always was. That was our normal.

DOI: 10.4324/9781003202141-1

It is possible that I do not remember when my father went to prison because he served two sentences before I reached middle school. I imagine that when a parent is incarcerated when a child is so young, their memories of the event may be few and far between depending on the circumstances. That is the case for me with my father's prior sentences. I know it happened, but I cannot remember who told me or how I felt. When I look at the picture in my grandmother's house, I often search my face for some indication of how I was feeling at the time. I look happy enough. There is a slight smile on my face, but I never could discern the full story. I have also never asked. I could ask my grandmother, who at 75 still has enough energy to entertain her great-grandchildren and attend church regularly in her best hat, but I never do. Sometimes, I think it may be too painful of a period for her to discuss. Our family changed drastically during my father's incarceration, which is not uncommon. Time waits for no one. Both of my father's paternal grandparents died while he was incarcerated. My great-grandfather passed when I was in high school. He was an extraordinary man. He attended Howard University and was stationed in Europe during WWII. He was a reverend in the local church and was devoted to my great-grandmother for over 60 years. They lived together without assistance until he was over 90 years old. When he died, my great-grandmother's health began to deteriorate and without her partner she could no longer live alone. She died when I was a freshman in college. My father was not granted permission to attend the funeral of either of his grandparents. In 2010, my father's sister took her own life in while my father was still in prison. Although she was his only sibling, he was not granted permission to attend this funeral either. While it was difficult to go through these challenging family times without my father, he did not just miss solemn occasions, but happy ones as well. For over 20 years, he was not physically present for birthdays, graduations, weddings, or births. He was also absent for small moments. He wasn't there to put money under our pillows for the tooth we lost, watch our face light up on Christmas morning, or comfort us after a trying day at school. While I remember the big events he missed more vividly, it is that small day-to-day moments where he seemed most absent. Everyone grieved his absence in their own way. My mother had already moved on with her life, but still remained angry about having to raise three children alone, a burden that still weighs on her today. My younger brother created illusions of what life would be like if our father was home and it was quite different than the life we were actually living. However, the person who mourned my father the most was his mother.

For over 30 years, my grandmother has been separated from one of her children. One by prison and another by suicide. It is now impossible that they will ever be back together as a familial unit. She was not able to see her children together outside of prison walls since the 1990s. She will never be able to recreate that picture that ignites so many thoughts in my mind. Sometimes I wonder if I am making excuses about the reason I choose not to discuss the photograph with my grandmother. I may not be protecting her, but instead protecting myself. It may be me who does not want to discuss the picture. It is an odd thought for me to ponder because for the past four years I have been called on numerous times to speak to groups of complete strangers about my father's incarceration and I am happy to do so. It feels good to share my story with others. In that space, I feel like I have control. In that space, I feel impactful. In that space, I can separate the story from the pain. I have extracted a version of my story meant for public consumption. It is a real part of my story, but it is free from emotion, the result of years of practice where I mostly ignored my father's incarceration in order to function daily. I learned to cope, as the youth I collaborated with during my study did as well. None of our stories were exactly the same. None of us had the same precise set of circumstances, reactions, or strategies for dealing with parental incarceration, but one thing we did have in common was the ability and desire to continue living our lives. In the early days of my father's last prison sentence, I did not know exactly what it was going to look like to continue living my life. It was not something I planned out; it was something I just knew I had to do. However, even with that understanding, it was a long and difficult process.

My most vivid memories of my father are from his last sentence. Prior to that, I have some vague memories of my mother and father arguing, us (my mother and brothers) moving a few times and seeing my father on an infrequent basis. Sometimes he would drive his truck over to our house and take me down the street to get something to eat. Other times, he may just call me to come outside while he stayed in his vehicle. My father always loved cars. He still does. When we were younger, he drove a Chevy Camaro which felt like the coolest car. As I got older, he usually drove a pickup truck that he used for his landscaping business. I remember one time I was in the house and he called me to come outside. He had brought me a ten-pound bag of white rice because he heard that's what I enjoyed eating. At the time, I was unimpressed with the gesture, but now I recognize it as a sign of parental love. The truth is I was already somewhat disenchanted with my father by this time. I remember him here and there throughout my earliest years, but I wouldn't call him a consistent presence. Maybe I cannot remember when he was consistently there because I was too young. I do, however, remember that when I was ten or eleven years old, my mother informed me my father was back in jail. At the time, I was unfamiliar with the term recidivism and how common it was. Again, this was not the first time he was incarcerated, but it is the first time I remember being told and old enough to comprehend what was happening. I was not privy to the details of the alleged crime nor was I present at the trial. I did not receive much information except that my father was incarcerated for a third time. It was a confusing time. I was hearing the adults in my world say things like "three strikes" and "kingpin charges," but I did not understand what it meant. I would later find out that he was sentenced to 22 years in federal prison. I was not even a teenager yet, so at the time 22 years seemed like a lifetime. In fact, it was double the amount of time I had been on Earth at that point. When I heard the news, I felt a sort of numbness that I still recognize within myself today. Inside, the small piece of hope that I had that he would not leave again died. When my father began to call from prison, I initially accepted the calls out of a sense of duty and respect. He often called early in the morning when my younger brother and I were getting ready for school. My mother worked the overnight shift and she was not usually home at this time. Their contentious relationship was nonexistent by this point and continues to be strained today. My older brother had his own life and as a teen had no interest in being roused from his sleep to talk on the phone. My younger brother seemed to be taking my father's incarceration harder than I was. It felt like it fell on me to maintain communication. In my sleepy state, I would engage in what felt like superficial conversation. I would explain what I was doing, but felt awkward asking the same. My father would ask me about school and life and I would answer with what has become my characteristic nonchalance. However, when I got off the phone I would cry. In my mind, I would think *if he loved me, he wouldn't have left me.* This would set the tone for my day. Eventually I stopped answering the calls so I could ignore the pain instead of working through it. No one in my household pressured me to keep answering because they had already separated themselves from the responsibility of maintaining a relationship with my father and I did not see the point of continuing something that seemed to cause me pain. I was angry and hurting and I did not know what to do with those feelings. I also felt a lot of guilt. Recently I was discussing the relationship between those who are incarcerated and their loved ones on the outside with a friend who was also directly impacted by incarceration and how common it is for loved ones to feel a sense of guilt in relation to an incarcerated individual. If you miss a call, you feel guilty because you know how much they look forward to speaking with someone. If there is a big event or occasion, you may downplay it in order to spare their feelings. I had long been searching for a way to explain this guilt and the most relevant term I could think of was survivor's guilt. While I was not with my father during any of the events leading up to or during his arrest, I still felt guilty that he was incarcerated and I was in society free to live my life. Although I was unaware of it at the time, a 2005 report from the Urban Institutes' Justice Policy Center identified survivor's guilt as one of the possible effects of separation due to incarceration. This guilt and my inability to explain it hindered my relationship with my father for a long time. However, I did find other places to channel my energy.

At school, I exceled. Being a good student became my identity to a detrimental extent. Some studies about children of incarcerated parents (COIP) highlight the difficulties they may have in school, but my experience was the opposite. I had always enjoyed school because formal education had come quite naturally to me. By middle school however, it had become who I was. I had to be in the highest-level class. I had to participate in the gifted programs. *Yes,* I would think to myself, *my family does not have a lot of money and my father is in prison, but I am not a stereotype.* I was obsessed with achieving. Good grades made me feel worthy. It was as if I knew the world was currently or was going to be judging me and I had to prepare to refute anything anyone said through my stellar grades and behavior. For the most part, it worked. I never remember a single teacher questioning me about my father's absence. Instead, report cards and parent teacher conferences were happy events where my mother could feel proud and I could get the external validation I desperately sought. However, there were cracks in this veneer. In 6th grade, I received a "B+" in science. While most children might be happy with this mark, I was in shambles. I cried and cried, which resulted in my mother eventually scheduling a sit down with the teacher. He concluded that he graded something improperly and raised my grade to an A minus. It was not perfect, but at least it was an A. I am still unsure if the teacher actually made a mistake or if he was just attempting to be kind because I was so distraught. As an educator, I know it is possible for teachers to make an error. I believe it is also possible that he was willing to give me a few more points in an attempt to calm my distress. Anyone who witnessed me at the time could easily see that this grade meant more to me than just a letter on a piece of paper. These grades were how I contributed to making my mother's life easier and it lessened my own sense of unworthiness. By high school, I learned to appear calm concerning my grades. I still took high-level courses and inwardly stressed about my performance, but I also developed more of a social life. It was not necessarily uncool to be smart, but it was uncool to be obsessively worried about every assignment or grade. I still did quite well, but I learned to produce an outward countenance that was more comforting to people, an act I now recognize as emotional labor which we will discuss in more detail later. Even though I became less outwardly focused on grades, the inner desire for approval was still there. I stopped trying as hard so I would not be upset if I did not get the grade I wanted, but still managed to graduate high school with a near perfect average. I even finished school a semester early, but instead of going to community college for a semester to earn some credits toward my future degree, I decided to work. Had I known what I know now about course loads and the cost of credits, it would have been more financially beneficial to attend community college for a semester, I was navigating a lot of these things on my own. Everything was new to me and I stumbled a lot as I tried to make the jump from high-performing high school student to college freshman. For my brothers, school did not provide the same validation. While both are highly intelligent, they eventually left traditional schooling prior to receiving their high school diplomas. School was not their coping mechanism and they found their solace in other areas.

I aspired to go to college for a long time. There was no question in my mind that I would attend a four-year university once I graduated. However, I had little knowledge about the business of college. I heard that my great-grandfather graduated from Howard University in Washington, D.C., known to many in the United States as the Black Harvard and now most famous for being the alma mater of Vice President, Kamala Harris, but that seemed like ancient history to me. Plus, by the time I reached the age to apply to college, my great-grandfather was already deceased. My lack of knowledge about college is now very clear to me as an adult. I had excellent grades, but they could have been better if I applied myself. I did not participate in many extracurricular activities because I was more interested in spending time with my friends. I had enough credits to graduate early and attend community college, but it cost money so I just decided to spend that time working at CVS (Customer Value Store) instead. I applied to schools by myself since my family was not well versed in the process and my school guidance counselor did not seem to have a strong belief in my capabilities despite my grades. When it came time to choose a college,

I shunned my great-grandfather's alma mater to head to New York City, attracted to its cosmopolitan reputation. While these may all seem like normal teenage transgressions, what I notice looking back is a person who was teetering between two worlds. On the one hand, I needed to be exceptional to shake off these things that I felt made people view me with disdain; being Black and poor, coming from a single parent household, and having a parent and, by this point, a brother in prison. On the other hand, I could not shake this feeling of unworthiness, which outside of school caused me to engage in risky and often self-destructive behaviors. I needed help to balance myself, the steady hand of some sort of guidance, but not many noticed my struggle because I was succeeding academically.

When I became an educator, a career I considered after I realized that the newspaper style journalism I majored in during college was not for me; I did not imagine that my father's incarceration would be a factor in my role as a teacher. However, it did not take long before it crept in. It started innocently. The children, who were in elementary school at the time, were fascinated with my life outside of school. I found it heartwarming because I remembered the feeling when you discover your teacher is more than just your teacher. It is astonishing to learn that they have a first name, a home outside of school and often have a partner and/or children. For me, it was Mrs. B. She was a gentle woman who encouraged my love of reading. I was certain that her whole life was devoted to me and to a lesser degree, the other children in my elementary school. One day when I was strolling through the neighborhood I noticed her in the backyard of a brick house tending a garden. I was so confused. I thought she lived at school! When I stopped to speak with her, she mentioned that her son was home from college. A son? I was shocked that I did not know this. Immediately after our conversation I went home to report this new information to my mother who understandably was less astounded than I was. While many things in education have changed since I was in elementary school, the children's fascination with their teacher has not. I fielded lots of questions about my life with each new class. *Who did I live with?* By myself. *Where's your mom?* She lives in a different state. *Where's your dad?* He's in prison. *Who takes care of you when you are sick?* My friends help me. The children asked countless questions, but they did not skip a beat when I said my father was in prison. I answered the question honestly because I did not see a reason to conceal the truth. I was not attempting to be an advocate at the time although these conversations would eventually lead me on that journey. To me, it was simply the truth and while they did not need to know details (and to their credit – never asked for them), answering honestly was just a natural reflex. It had been that way for as long as I can remember. I did not always volunteer the information, but if asked, I was honest. One of topics I will discuss later in this book is stigma and shame, two issues that I feel are not explored with enough nuance when related to children of incarcerated parents. While my story is unique to me, I never remember feeling ashamed of my father. I did have an acute understanding that others may find it shameful and judge me. I understood that people assumed or thought I should feel ashamed. In response to this understanding, I chose silence until asked and once asked, I chose transparency. I do not know how it got back to the administration at my school, but one day, my well-intentioned assistant principal approached me and informed me that I should reconsider telling people about my incarcerated father because they may view me differently. It was in this moment, all that I knew was true, but could never prove, was validated. People were judging me and all the work I had done to become a successful professional did not stop that. I thanked her for the advice, but decided not to take it. By this time, one of my students began to share with me that his father was incarcerated too. Sometimes he would bring in drawings his father sent him and he would share them with me. He saved all of things his father sent him, something that I found to be common among the youth I collaborated with as well. These interactions with my student brought back memories of the cards I received for birthdays or graduations, carefully drawn by the resident artist that was incarcerated with my father. When I was younger, I thought that my dad drew these pictures. For a while, I even thought that everyone who goes to jail or prison must have the time to become a skilled artist. It was not until I was older that I realized that my dad was paying someone to draw these cards for him, almost the same way I stop by a local pharmacy to buy a card before a party. Except these cards were more special because they were not mass produced. My student and I were both able to find some joy in the fact that our parents had cared enough to have a custom card made for us and that our name was a part of the card design instead of being added to it later.

Knowing that my student had an incarcerated parent was important to me as an educator. It made me make more conscious decisions about my language and teaching style. Many teachers ask students to make cards throughout the year for their parents. This seems like a fun and thoughtful activity, but for students dealing with parental separation, it can be a difficult and stressful task. Things that seemed routine to me before, now required closer examination. I began to read more about parental incarceration, ostensibly to learn how to support my students, but also to learn more about myself as well. The numbers shocked me. There were millions of children in the United States, who were currently dealing with or previously had dealt with parental incarceration. I could not understand why I had never heard it mentioned during my time working in the school system. This was particularly puzzling considering that I worked in the largest school system in the United States and that if New York were its own country, it would be the world's fifth largest incarcerator (Prison Policy Initiative, 2021). I did not hear anyone discuss parental incarceration at professional development conferences, nor did I not see it represented in social emotional curriculums, and I could not find a book in the entire school library that touched upon the topic at all. It was just not discussed. As a special education teacher, I had access to my children's social histories. Occasionally while reading through the documents, I would see that one of my students had an incarcerated parent. I found this information helpful, but I was also dismayed that I was only able to obtain it because the student was in special education. I strongly felt that in order for educators to best support their students, having some awareness and knowledge of parental incarceration was important. I still deeply believe that, but I now have a better understanding of why this is not an easy task.

I decided to go back to school for my PhD in my mid-twenties. School is where I felt the safest; the place where I received the validation I desired. Now not only did I work in one, but completing my PhD meant that I would spend a large portion of my personal time devoted to education and schooling as well. I was in a small cohort of students (less than 20) in what was probably the most diverse classroom I had ever been a part of. While many of the professors were white, which is still commonplace in higher education, my cohort was mostly people of color who made me feel at home and secure in a setting which otherwise would have been very intimidating. On our first day of classes, we were asked to share a prospective research topic with the class. Our professor made sure to let us know that these were just ideas and that it was quite common for people to change their research interests throughout their doctoral journey. I was the last person to share so I had the opportunity to listen to all of the important topics my peers were interested in pursuing. My anxiety built as we went around the circle. In my heart, I knew I wanted to research children of incarcerated parents, but I was unsure if it was a topic worthy of research. I knew my family and I had dealt with it, as well as a few of my students, but I never heard anyone else talk about it. When it was my turn, I took the safe route and stated I wanted to study standardized testing and students in special education. I could tell from the reactions that it was considered a suitable topic. People nodded and affirmed my choice. It was not an amazing reaction, but at least it fit. It did not call attention to the fact that I was not sure I belonged there and I was grappling with imposter syndrome on day one. I waited a second, disappointed in the fact that I only felt comfortable using my voice when it felt safe, something I actively struggle with today. However, this time was different, and I pushed the words out of my mouth and into the ears of my peers. *Or maybe children of incarcerated parents and how they perform in school.* I added the latter part (school performance) to fulfill what I thought was the education requirement of the Urban Education program. Almost immediately I heard murmurs around the room. The consensus was that this was an important topic, a topic that needed more research and exploration and a topic that I should pursue. Inside I smiled. While our professor was correct that it was normal for research interests to change, or develop over time, I never changed my topic. It was important to me on a personal and professional level and because of my passion for the topic, my commitment to it never wavered.

As I began to work on the literature review necessary for my dissertation, I started to notice some patterns developing. While literature reviews are meant to be exhaustive, I cannot claim to have read every single book or article about or related to children of incarcerated parents. I did, however, explore numerous studies, articles, and books related to the topic. The results shocked me. Initially, I was pleased to learn that there even was literature on the topic of not only children of incarcerated parents, but mass incarceration as a whole. As nonsensical as it may sound, I had gone my whole life without knowing that I had a community. The literature I was reading and analyzing proved that I had one, but now I had to face what some of the literature was saying about my newfound community. I read articles that described children of incarcerated parent's anti-social behaviors, poor intellectual outcomes and propensity for drug use and imprisonment. I felt torn. I experienced parental incarceration for most my life, yet I had not gone to prison. I was in a doctoral program and considered myself intelligent. The story being told in those articles was not my story, but that didn't mean it wasn't someone's story. In fact, despite my aversion to incarceration, by this time both of my brothers had been incarcerated. I considered that perhaps the studies were correct and I was the exception to the rule, but that felt arrogant and improbable. While one narrative seemed to appear in almost every article, the one where COIP are vulnerable children at risk for numerous negative outcomes, I barely saw the other one. The story where the child adjusts, perseveres, and thrives or at least functions. One thing that I will always credit my doctoral program with is providing me the tools and confidence to critically analyze research. I grew up in an era where Jay-Z was king and he once stated, "Men lie. Women lie. Numbers don't." This quote sums up how I used to view research. I thought of it as this totally objective undertaking where the results were simply facts. However, I quickly learned that (1) not all quality research involves numerical calculations, (2) numbers and findings can and often are presented in ways to support certain narratives, and (3) nothing involving humans is entirely objective. I stopped reading research as absolute truth and started to explore the story it was trying to tell and why it was interested in telling that particular story. I began to ponder what part of the larger narrative about COIP does each study, each article, each book, and each Op-Ed fit into and as I did that my study began to form. Because so much of what I was reading fell into a larger narrative about children of incarcerated parents and adverse outcomes, I began to think about why the information was being presented in this way. While almost no one views parental incarceration as a positive event, myself included, I still wondered why weren't there any stories about children of incarcerated parents who were doing quite well, at least by societal standards of success? That question was at least partially answered for me as I became immersed in the world of portraiture while reading *The Art and Science of Portraitures* (1997) by Sara Lawrence-Lightfoot and Jessica Hoffman Davis. At the time of my doctoral education, the book was almost 20 years old, but it provided me with the words to explain what appeared to be happening in the research I was reviewing. No book or quote had a greater influence on the formation of my study than this excerpt:

> I was concerned, for example, about the general tendency of social scientists to focus their investigations on pathology and disease rather than on health and resilience. This general propensity is magnified in the research on education and schooling, where investigators have been much more vigilant in documenting failure than they have been in describing examples of success. To some extent the focus on pathology is understandable, maybe even laudable. Certainly some investigators have identified things that do not work, or work poorly, as a prelude to trying to figure out ways of fixing what is broken…But the relentless scrutiny of failure has many unfortunate and distorting results.
>
> (pp. 7–8)

In a polite, but forceful way, Lawrence-Lightfoot and Davis confronted the harm of an extreme focus on failure, notably that this focus often ends in a "blaming of the victim." For me this was key. I had read so many articles about bad grades, poor behavior, and broken homes, but few with a clear focus on the structural inequalities that cause many children, not just COIP, to have difficulty in schools, other institutions and at times society in general. I had read even fewer that instead chose to look at the "examples of success" that Lawrence-Lightfoot and Davis mentioned. Lawrence-Lightfoot and Davis were forgiving, asserting that most investigators were well-intentioned and perhaps should even be celebrated for their attention to and attempts to fix what is broken. As a biracial Black woman reading the book 20 years later, I wasn't ready to call these efforts laudable. In my view, children of incarcerated parents weren't broken. Their parents weren't broken. Their families weren't broken. It wasn't laudable to try to emphasize the difficulties of these children and families without examining the brokenness of our society; a policing structure birthed from the hunting of enslaved people; a criminal justice system that marginalizes Black people and other groups including immigrants, LGBTQ+, disabled people, and poor people; and a school system that often replicates the racism, sexism, elitism, and xenophobia occurring in society. Lawrence-Lightfoot and Davis gave me not only the words, but also the methodological foundation to state that I was interested in documenting success and health. I wanted to create portraits of COIP that were complex and nuanced, what Lawrence-Lightfoot and Davis (1997) refer to as the "coexistence of strengths and vulnerabilities (p.8)." However, I did not want to create these portraits as an observer from a distance. Instead, I wanted to engage in the collaborative creation with COIP, allowing their words to form the picture of whom each individual was as a whole, not just as the child of an incarcerated parent. I felt my background was vital to this endeavor.

During my doctoral studies, we discussed the positionality of the researcher and their status as an "insider" or "outsider." Insider status meant that the investigator was a part of the community they were researching. An outsider status meant that the investigator was not part of the community or had no meaningful connections to the community. When I began my research, I was firmly in the insider category. My father was still incarcerated and had been for over a decade. In the world of academia where objectivity, or at least the illusion of it, was the gold standard, I wasn't sure if being an insider was a positive label. However, in hindsight, I believe it truly was an asset and a gift. Much has been written about the need to reform traditional notions of research and decolonize Eurocentric research methodologies. While I didn't know how to name it at the time, that decolonization of research was vital to my role of an investigator. As Keikelame and Swartz (2019) write, "A decolonising research methodology is an approach that is used to challenge the Eurocentric research methods that undermine the local knowledge and experiences of the marginalised population groups" (p. 1). While Keikelame and Swartz were discussing a research project in South Africa and referring to the historical methods of research where investigators observed and analyzed people using their supposedly superior or civilized worldview, I could not help but apply this to my own study. From what I was reading, many studies seemed to be conducted by outsiders looking for a problem instead of a solution and the problem was usually with child, the incarcerated parent or the family as a whole instead of any of the systems that support and perpetuate mass incarceration in this country. I read far too many studies about COIP that discussed them, but didn't include their voices. I knew I wanted to highlight their "local knowledge and experiences" or what I refer to as lived expertise. Decolonizing research also argues that "issues of power, trust, culture and cultural competence, respectful and legitimate research practice and recognition of individual and communities' assets are important structures to be considered in a decolonising process" (p. 3). The outcome of decolonizing research can often be action toward social justice. All of this appealed to me as an investigator, but also as the child of an incarcerated parent. I wanted the power between myself and my collaborators to be as balanced as possible. Although I was conducting the research, they were and remain the holders of knowledge and narrators of their own stories. I also felt that trust was key to conducting valuable research. Marginalized groups have often been used as research subjects without any real input or value added to their communities. This, among other issues, can sometimes lead to a lack of trust between the investigator(s) and the people participating in the study. Because parental incarceration is such a personal topic, establishing a level of trust was imperative to obtaining the complex information I was seeking. I decided to earn the trust of my participants through authenticity and transparency. I was fortunate to have a truly wonderful dissertation committee, who although they were not directly impacted (or at minimum have never shared that they were) understood my vision and provided me with invaluable support. Some of this support included connecting me with Dr. Kathy Boudin, a formerly incarcerated advocate who is now the Co-Director and Co-Founder of the Center for Justice at Columbia University. She is also mother to Chesa Boudin, the District Attorney of San Francisco who has been implementing major criminal justice reforms in that city. I firmly believe that Chesa's experience as the child of an incarcerated parent influences his zeal for reform and progress. While she may not recall the assistance she provided to me, Dr. Boudin connected me to the Osborne Association and is partially responsible for kindling my career as a public speaker on the topic of parental incarceration.

Recruiting from an organization that was already doing work with children of incarcerated parents was a practical move. Because many people do not talk about their loved ones incarceration to outsiders, it is difficult to determine who may or may not have an incarcerated parent and making assumptions is not suggested. By connecting with an organization already dedicated to directly impacted individuals, I knew that I would have access to youth who publicly acknowledged their parent's incarceration and were already willing to speak about it to a certain extent. However, it was paramount to me that I did not use the organization for my own purposes and leave. I began attending meetings so that people would become more familiar with me. I drove from Brooklyn to Queens a few times to make myself a presence at the Osborne Association. However, recruitment was still slow and difficult. I had given birth less than a year prior and felt torn between being a mom and being a researcher. Eventually, the Osborne Association asked to speak at an event dedicated to supporting young children with an incarcerated parent. I had never considered myself a public speaker although I did not have an aversion to it. I had come to gather stories, but hadn't considered that some may want to hear mine. Instead of doing research, I started to do events. At first I was just happy that people wanted to hear my story. However, something amazing began to happen. As I shared my story, including my journey to my doctoral program, people began approaching me to have their children participate in my study. I won't make it seem like it was an astronomical number of people, but it was enough to conduct the type of nuanced research I planned. The people who approached me did not do so for their own gain. Participating in the study did not provide the youth or their parents/caregivers with any tangible benefit. However, by sharing my story I had earned their trust and they felt comfortable that I was not attempting to exploit or marginalize their child. Instead, I was interested in highlighting and uplifting the good while presenting COIP as fully dimensional beings.

My father was released in time to attend my son's first birthday party. When I walked the stage to accept my doctorate, it was the first graduation of mine that he was able to attend. Our relationship has progressed slowly since the days I refused to answer his phone calls. When he first came home, I chose not to make the four-hour drive to the party my grandmother hosted in his honor. I had other plans and an infant I was caring for alone. I refused to inconvenience myself yet I still felt guilty. My guilt was somewhat lessened when I spoke to my father on the phone and realized he found the party overwhelming. We are similar in that way. Being social exhausts us. In a weird way, I felt more connected to him by not attending, than I probably would have if I had resentfully chosen to attend. While our relationship still isn't perfect, it is much better and I credit my son for that. Becoming a mother humbled me and I realized the mistakes we make as parents are not a reflection of the love we have for our children, but instead usually a result of us searching for the love we are supposed to have for ourselves. I can now empathize with my father. I cannot imagine the pain it would cause to be separated from my child and the devastation I would feel if he refused my calls. In the less than five years that my son has been on this Earth, I have erred, but I have never stopped loving him. This is the way I now choose to see my father. Like any other parent, he was not perfect, but love does not require perfection.

This book too is borne out of love, but is not perfect. It is based on a small study that is nowhere near statistically relevant. For me, that is a point of celebration. For others, it may be a point of condemnation. The study took place in a very specific place (New York City) that is by no means representative of the remainder of the United States. I did not enter this study as an objective investigator, free from emotion. Instead, I entered with a deep attachment to and love for the community. And while I was open to wherever the data led, I was fully committed to highlighting the strengths of COIP. In fact, it's fair to say that I had an agenda. I aimed to provide a space where these youth, my collaborators, could share their lived expertise so that we could be a part of changing the narrative about our community. This book is the continuation of that journey. It is not a large edited edition that collects research and think pieces from the top people in the field. Those books exist. They serve a purpose. They are warranted. This book, however, is different. It is a collection of the voices of directly impacted people, myself included, who want others to realize that people who have experienced parental incarceration are experts on the topic as well. They are the holders of knowledge; knowledge that they so graciously shared with me and I am now able to share with you. I encourage you to accept their gift with not only an open mind, but also an open heart. Their words are not just research or data; they are also change and love. They have given us their stories so that we may better know how to care for those who come after them. They have shared their knowledge so that we can develop the tools to dismantle the challenges and obstacles that so many face. Their gift is now our work. Let's begin.

References

Keikelame, M.J. & Swartz, L. (2019). Decolonising research methodologies: lessons from a qualitative research project, Cape Town, South Africa. *Global Health Action*, 12(1), 1–7.

Lawrence-Lightfoot, S., & Davis J. (1997). *The art and science of portraiture.* San Francisco, CA: Jossey-Bass.

Prison Policy Initiative. (2021). *United States profile.* Northampton, MA. https://www.prisonpolicy.org/contact.html

1 Challenging Deficit-Based Views of Children of Incarcerated Parents

The State of Research

Scientific research has been used to make the world a better place and remedy numerous challenges. It has also been used as a justification for racism, sexism and several other forms of discrimination. While highlighting the inherent value of quality research, we must also acknowledge the ways research has been weaponized against oppressed communities. We simply cannot pretend that the pervasive racism present in society, both historically and currently, has no influence on the way researchers investigate certain topics and people.

(Whitney Q. Hollins)

In 2012 Farrington et al. stated:

The number of children experiencing parental incarceration in countries like the United States is unprecedented. Identifying and understanding the possible effects on children is of great importance... Relatively little is known about the causal effects of parental incarceration on children. This topic warrants large-scale investment...

(p. 193)

In the decade that has passed since their assertion, much has changed while some things have remained the same. The United States still holds the unenviable title as world's leading incarcerator, with 2.2 million individuals currently incarcerated and an additional 4.7 under some sort of legal surveillance (Sykes & Pettit, 2019). This figure represents a 500% increase in the last 40 years (The Sentencing Project, 2020). Since the United States has a sizable number of currently or formerly incarcerated individuals, it also has a staggering number of children who are currently experiencing or previously experienced parental incarceration. It is estimated that more than 5 million children

DOI: 10.4324/9781003202141-2

in the United States under the age of 14 have experienced separation from a co-resident parent due to incarceration. This figure equates to approximately 7% of all children in the United States (Murphey & Cooper, 2015). Eddy and Poehlmann (2019) note that this figure most likely underestimates the number of children impacted by parental incarceration because it does not account for the children affected by the incarceration of a nonresident parent. For example, I would not have been included in this figure because I did not live with my father at the time of his incarceration. Without the inclusion of those children the figure is still astonishing. With their inclusion, it is difficult to imagine just how many children have been impacted by parental incarceration prior to age 18. While we can no longer view the number of children experiencing parental incarceration, at least in the United States, as "unprecedented," it is still shocking. I recall viewing my father's incarceration as a very personal experience. I did not know of any other families who were impacted by incarceration in the same way that I was as I was growing up in a small town in Maryland. I now know that this is highly unlikely. There were most likely other children in my town impacted in the same way as my siblings and I were, I was just unaware that they existed. Despite a decade passing, it is still true that relatively little is known about the causal effects of parental incarceration on children. I doubt this will change anytime within the near future because while there are an increasing number of studies that seek to examine the effects of parental incarceration on children, it is nearly impossible to undoubtedly establish parental incarceration as the cause of these effects. Acknowledging this, Besemer et al. (2019) state:

> Although the outcomes associated with parental imprisonment are well-established, there remains uncertainty about their cause. High levels of disadvantages in the families of prisoners make it difficult to identify whether negative outcomes are a consequence of parental imprisonment itself or a reflection of children's greater exposure to pre-existing and concurrent risk factors.
>
> (p. 65)

The outcomes associated with parental incarceration are correlative and not causative. While any outcomes determined from research are still valuable, it is important to note that parental incarceration has not been determined to be the sole cause of any adverse outcome. Despite this, it also remains that identifying the effects of parental incarceration is a topic that warrants large-scale investment and to a certain extent this has happened. Between 2012 and 2016, there were

260 new publications concerning parental incarceration and children of incarcerated parents (Scharff Smith, 2019). The fact that more attention is being paid to parental incarceration and its effects on children is a positive development. However, the emphasis should not strictly be on the number of studies or publications, but also on what the publications and research add to the community. When I began the literature review for my study in 2014, right in the middle of the publication boom, I was dismayed to find several studies that were problem-focused. At the time my father was still incarcerated and reading some of the publications felt like an attack; on my family, on my father, and on me and my future. The emphasis on the problems children of incarcerated parents will face has been noticed by other researchers as well. In a rallying call for more resilience based research, Shlafer et al. (2019) state, "The research that has emerged within the past decade has provided important information to the development of children and adolescents with incarcerated parents. However, this research has been overwhelmingly problem-focused" (p. 112). While examining the issues children of incarcerated parents may experience is important, an extreme focus on problems can be detrimental to the community. For example, if the research is searching for problems and is consistently publishing that children of incarcerated parents experience certain adverse outcomes, it reinforces the notion that this population is broken or damaged. When compounded with the fact that children of incarcerated parents are likely to already experience other forms of marginalization due to their race or socio-economic status, this problem-based focus is harmful. As Bruns and Lee (2019) state, "To be sure, mass incarceration is not the only racialized system impacting racial/ethnic minority families. Due to the long history of discrimination in the USA, these families also face assaults from other institutions and experience co-occurring disadvantages" (p. 39). While some may argue that research is objective and the findings are as well, structural racism is present within research and academia. I would argue that research institutions can also be places where people and families of color experience disadvantages. This is not to say that all problem-based research is rooted in racism or elitism, but when certain groups are consistently studied by people seeking to find what is wrong with them, investigators must examine why such a one-sided approach is being implemented. This is especially true of children of incarcerated parents because race and the criminal justice system are enmeshed. While research has been diligent in pointing out the racial and economic disproportionately present in jails and prisons and how this, in turn, presents itself in the demographics of children

of incarcerated parents, investigators have been less cognizant about how the framework of their research can reinforce the stereotypes that help support the carceral apparatus.

Research Prior to 2012

Prior to 2012 there was an emerging body of literature devoted to children of incarcerated parents, but there was not nearly as much current research about the population as there is today. In this section, I will give two examples of literature that influenced my decision to conduct my study in the way I did. *All Alone in the World* (2005) provided an intimate window into the experiences of children impacted by parental incarceration. Even as the child of an incarcerated parent, I was shocked to read about children who were left to fend for themselves after the arrest of a parent. I was not present when my father was arrested and it was hard for me to fathom that officers would enter a home and arrest a parent, without planning for their minor children. Since the publication of this book, many states have pushed for sensitive arrest policies and in 2014 the International Association of Chiefs of Police published a report titled *Safeguarding Children of Arrested Parents*. Reading this book provided me with my first glimpse of just how powerful the stories of children of incarcerated parents were. While Bernstein made several points that were back by empirical data, it was the supporting stories that captured my attention. I decided that I too wanted to forefront the voices of children with incarcerated parents in whatever I wrote. Another publication that had an influence on my study formation was research published by Julie Poehlmann in 2005. Poehlmann's study is titled *Children's Family Environments and Intellectual Outcomes During Maternal Incarceration* that sought to highlight the exponentially increasing number of incarcerated mothers and the effects their incarceration had on their children. Poehlmann, a highly respected clinical psychologist and researcher, has decades of experience in the field and remains a leading expert. When I first found this study during my doctoral studies, I was drawn in by the title and discovered that part of the study included the use of the Sanford-Binet Intelligence Scale to measure intellectual outcomes. As a special education teacher I was familiar with the scale, although I had never administered it myself. Nonetheless, I was privy to the ways the score could and sometimes did change throughout a child's academic career depending on circumstances such as the person administering the test and the mood of the child. Even more, I was aware of research that analyzed the racial gap between Black and Latinx children and their white counterparts. While some people use this research to support white supremacist claims that white people are genetically superior, others have used it implore people to view the test in a different light. Lindsey (2013) described these opposing views when discussing a study by Heritage Foundation Scholar Jason Richwine in which Richwine used IQ scores to support his theory that American "Hispanics" are less intelligent than native-born white people. Lindsey wrote:

> Jason Richwine is the latest exemplar of the so-called "hereditarian" interpretation of IQ – namely, that IQ scores are a reliable indicator of immutable, inborn intelligence across all groups of people, and therefore that group differences in IQ indicate group differences in native intelligence. Yes, the hereditarian view lends aid and comfort to racists and nativists. But more importantly, it's just plain wrong. Specifically, it is based on the ahistorical and ethnocentric assumption of a fixed relationship between the development of certain cognitive skills and raw mental ability. In truth, the skills associated with intelligence have changed over time – and unevenly through social space – as society evolves.
>
> (p. 1)

Poehlmann's study did not use IQ to support racist ideology and the study found that in this particular investigation, racial-ethnic status "did not emerge as a significant predictor in any analysis" (p. 1282). And while that may be true, I have trouble removing the framework of race from a test originally designed by European scientists for European children that has been adapted to meet American measures of intelligence. This is especially true considering that structural factors have excluded certain groups in this country from a certain quality of life en masse and that this exclusion has affected the mental, physical, and emotional health of certain Americans for hundreds of years. I wish there was a stronger critique of the test within this study. The Sanford-Binet Intelligence Scale can provide valuable information about the skillset of a person, but it should also come with a disclaimer that it is not immune to the effects of systemic racism. Because children of incarcerated parents are overwhelming children of color, this context is important. Poehlmann's study acknowledges that intellectual outcomes can be improved by lessening the amount of risks a child experiences. These risks include poverty and other sociodemographic factors. To improve the intellectual outcomes of children of incarcerated parents, Poehlmann suggests screening children at the time of their mother's incarceration and providing support to caregivers to make their living situation more stimulating, warm, and stable. While I believe in early intervention services, I do have my reservations about the implications of screening and tracking children of incarcerated parents. Often these initiatives begin with good intentions, but can spiral into harm. Children of incarcerated parents are disproportionately Black children. Screening them could further stigmatize and marginalize these children who already must deal with multiple layers of oppression. I agree that providing caregivers with support is extremely important and it is something that continues to be sorely lacking. However, there is a larger, structural issue present throughout the study that did not receive enough attention in my opinion. Poverty was mentioned a few times, but it is not enough to reactively lessen the poverty of caregivers. Proactive policies to alleviate poverty for all Americans would not only better support caregivers and children of incarcerated parents, it would also lower the incarceration rate and ensure that fewer parents are separated from their children in the first place. My fear at the time was that Poehlmann's study, despite her intentions and undoubtedly precise methods, could be utilized in the deficit-based narratives that further stigmatize children of incarcerated parents. I decided that I wanted to create a study where social justice and the acknowledgment of racism were the foundation. Working with children of incarcerated parents is not only a social justice issue, it is a structural racism issue. Working with children of incarcerated parents should be anti-racist work and researchers, particularly in the United States, should use critical race theory to examine the ways in which race, and specifically whiteness, influences the work they are doing.

Research on Intergenerational Criminality

Cesare Lombroso, considered to be the father of modern criminology, believed that certain people are born with an inclination to commit crimes. He believed that criminality could be hereditary and that this inherited passion for crime manifested itself physically. Lombroso described the features of a criminal, writing:

> Thus were explained anatomically the enormous jaws, high cheek bones, prominent superciliary arches, solitary lines in the palms, extreme size of the orbits, handle shaped or sessile ears found in criminals, savages and apes, insensibility to pain, extremely acute sight, tattooing, excessive idleness, love of orgies and the irresistible craving for evil for its own sake, the desire not only to

extinguish life in the victim, but to mutilate the corpse, tear its flesh, and drink its blood.

(Breterick, 2019, p. 1)

While many today would view Lombroso's theories as bizarre, his influence is still present in the way crime is presented and discussed in the U.S. His work is also proof that "science" isn't immune from the subjectivity and racism of the humans that employ it. The racism embedded in Lombroso's statement is clear. People of color have often been categorized as savages and Black people have historically been compared to apes and monkeys. An insensibility to pain is also a characteristic that has been used to justify heinous crimes against Black bodies, such as the experiments conducted by the father of gynecology, J. Marion Sims, who tortured enslaved women in the name of science. While Lombroso did acknowledge white criminality, he used the features of people of color as the representation of criminality. For example, he believed many male criminals exhibited "the projection of the lower face and jaws found in negroes" (Little, 2019). Charles A. Ellwood, a prominent American sociologist in the early 20th century, supported Lombroso's findings and thought that they should form the basis for the American criminal justice system (Little, 2019). Lombroso's work had a huge influence on criminology and other fields, and while few may make the connection today, it still seems to influence certain areas of research. For example, "the association between parental imprisonment and children's adulthood offending risk has been one of the oldest foci in parental incarceration literature" (Besemer et al., 2019, p. 67). While Lomborso theorized that criminality was genetic over a century ago, many researchers are still searching for an intergenerational crime link.

Those familiar with the field of criminal justice and specifically children of incarcerated parents have no doubt heard the statistic that children of incarcerated parents are 6 times more likely to be incarcerated as an adult than their non-impacted peers and that seven out of ten children of incarcerated parents will be imprisoned themselves at some point during their life. I most recently heard this statistic in 2019 while attending the National Children of Incarcerated Parents conference in Arizona. However, it was not the first time I heard or read this statistic and I have spent a considerable amount of attempting to trace it back to an empirical study, but have come up empty handed. Other people have investigated the claim as well. In 2009, the National Conference of States Legislatures wrote,

some claims about how parental incarceration affects children appear in the research, advocacy and policy literature might not be supported by empirical evidence. One such claim is that children of incarcerated parents are six times more likely than other children to be incarcerated as adults. No empirical data currently support this claim.

(Christian, p. 2)

Referencing the above statistics, Conway and Jones (2015) state,

These claims are dramatic and capture one's attention. They are also common on the internet, for example on websites of mentoring organizations intending to build support for resources to serve CIP. The figures are problematic because it is not at all clear that they are accurate.

(p. 5)

In an analysis of international research on the topic, Besemer et al. (2019) found:

Looking at findings across countries, it remains difficult to draw general conclusions regarding the effects of parental imprisonment on delinquency and offending in offspring…Overall, the results do not allow for any firm conclusions about the effects of imprisonment on children across countries in terms of delinquency and crime.

(pp. 70–71)

If the claims that children of incarcerated parents are six times more likely to be incarcerated as adults than their peers are unsubstantiated, it is worth exploring why it continues to be used and weaponized in the discussions about children of incarcerated parents. As I noted previously, Lawrence-Lightfoot and Davis (1997) were sympathetic to the desire of researchers to highlight problems within a certain population. It is possible, that in this vein, researchers are trying to highlight some of the challenges faced by children of incarcerated parents and therefore increase the amount of support they receive. However, Lawrence-Lightfoot and Davis (1997) also cautioned against this approach because it (1) led to victim-blaming and (2) made the situation appear so desperate that people felt there was little they could do to remedy it. While they weren't speaking specifically about children of incarcerated parents, their message resonates. Researchers should not be using an unsubstantiated statistic to elicit support for children of incarcerated parents. It actually may have the opposite effect.

As mentioned previously, people of color were the earliest references for Lombroso's genetic criminality theory; one which espoused that people are born criminals. Embedded in his theory is the position that people of color are more likely to be criminals. While Lombroso was an Italian criminologist, his work falls in line with how many Americans view people of color today. There are many people, as evidenced by the murders of Trayvon Martin and Ahmaud Arbery, who believe that Black is synonymous with criminal. They believe that they can tell by looking at someone if they are capable of committing a crime. Since children of incarcerated parents are disproportionately children of color, the focus on intergenerational criminality links can also be used to support racist practices in the criminal justice system. The consistent use of the erroneous finding that children of incarcerated parents are six times more likely to be incarcerated reinforces the notion of Black and brown criminality and positions children of incarcerated parents as a future threat to public safety. Research has shown that children of color in the United States, particularly Black children, are already viewed as more mature and threatening than their white counterparts (Henning, 2018; Laura, 2014). When these perceptions are coupled with the fact that children of incarcerated parents are disproportionately children of color, the use of this claim becomes harmful, if not dangerous. Framing children of incarcerated parents as future criminals does not stimulate support. It can instead support racist notions of people of color and take the onus away society's failings and place them squarely on the shoulders of Black and brown families.

It is also worth asking why the area of intergenerational crime is such a ripe area of interest for researchers in the first place? What sparked the idea that parents who have been incarcerated are more likely to have children who will be incarcerated at some point in their lives? Was it Lombroso's theory? Perhaps it was the desire that many of us to "see" danger in front of us. It can be frightening to live in a world where crime is portrayed as rampant and yet we have no clue who may commit a crime. It may offer some a sense of comfort for people to have some sort of indicator that someone may be potentially dangerous; whether it be physical appearance, upbringing, or genetics. To be clear, I do not believe that most people who state that children of incarcerated parents are more likely than their peers to be incarcerated today repeat this claim because they believe that people are born criminals. However, it cannot be overlooked that Lomborso's thoughts align with the thinking of some people in the United States who view people of color as deviants and threatening based solely on their appearance. Therefore, reinforcing this idea, especially without sound empirical data, is harmful. Researchers are perhaps searching for what would be one of the most devastating effects of parental incarceration of all; a cycle in which the parent's incarceration is the catalyst for their child's future imprisonment. However, in that theory, the blame also falls on the incarcerated parent instead of the structural inequities that help fill our jails, prisons, and detention centers. It is also possible that researchers looking for an intergenerational crime link want to do so for the purposes of highlighting the systemic factors that lead to incarceration. For example, most people in America tend to live within close to their childhood home. This is especially true for lower-income individuals with less formal education who may not have as many job opportunities or who may rely on their family for childcare (Bui & Miller, 2015). Research also shows that communities with higher poverty rates have higher rates of imprisonment (Rabuy & Kouf, 2015; Travis & Western, 2018). If children are growing up in the same impoverished communities as their parents, the incarceration of an adult children of incarcerated parents is not necessarily directly related to their parent's incarceration, but instead the concentrated disadvantage present in their community which could also be a factor in their parent's incarceration. There are many factors that are involved in a person's path to incarceration; some personal and many are structural. However, there is little empirical support for a casual effect between parental incarceration and the future incarceration of their child. If researchers are aware of this, they must abandon this narrative and question why there is such an emphasis on it to begin with.

Broken Families

Another area that numerous publications explore is the status of the family unit prior to parental incarceration. Numerous studies have shown that parental incarceration is typically not the first Adverse Childhood Experience (ACE) that the child of an incarcerated parent encounters. As Eddy and Kjellstrand (2011) state, "the incarceration of a family member is unlikely to mark the beginning of problems for a child and family" (p. 20). These ACEs include experiencing or witnessing violence or abuse, having a family member attempt to commit or die by suicide and growing up in a household where someone had substance abuse issues (Centers for Disease Control and Prevention, 2021). I found this to be true of my own experience and the youth I interviewed. However, it is important to note that ACEs are not just prevalent in the lives of children of incarcerated parents, but in the lives of Americans in general. The CDC reports that "ACEs are common. About 61% of adults surveyed across 25 states reported that they had experienced at least one type of ACE, and nearly 1 in 6 reported they had experienced four or more types of ACEs" (p. 1). While parental incarceration is an ACE, researchers should be clear when discussing the fact that while many children of incarcerated parents experience other ACEs prior to their parent's incarceration, this is not unique to children of incarcerated parents. The CDC also notes that "Some children are at greater risk than others. Women and several racial/ethnic minority groups were at greater risk for having experienced 4 or more types of ACEs" (p. 1). As a biracial Black woman, I was already more likely to experience ACEs than some of my peers, even without the incarceration of my father. Likewise, the youth I interviewed, who were all people of color, had all experienced one or more ACEs prior to their parent's incarceration. Vanessa, Delilah, and Amber grew up in a household where both parents had substance abuse issues. Orlando, Emmanuel, and Jacqueline recall witnessing their mother's being treated in disrespectful and sometimes abusive ways by their father. Emmanuel acknowledged this when discussing why it's unlikely his parents will reconnect due to his father's cheating and abuse despite his [Emmanuel's] wish that they would so.

> She [his mother] just takes us to visit. They're not really together. I can't lie, my dad really put my mom through a lot. I see why, even though I would want them, but I think my mom's making the right choice. I love my dad. He can be a great man, but he made the wrong decisions in life.

Despite maintaining a relationship with his dad, Emmanuel is still angry with him due to the way his father treated his mother. However Emmanuel said his father, whom he speaks with regularly, allows him to express his anger directly to him during their phone calls. Tres also has vivid memories of his parent's tumultuous relationship. He stated:

> The day I saw my mom and dad fight and my dad was on top of my mom and I was just sitting there and crying, I didn't know what to do. I just watched everything. I felt paralyzed. I wasn't. I was watching everything and everything was slow. I was just despised to see it.

Witnessing domestic violence left a long-lasting impression on Tres and he indicated that it caused him to dislike his father for a period of time.

He mentioned that his dislike for his father eventually lessened once he was incarcerated. This could be because with his father behind bars, Tres no longer had to witness the abuse of his mother. While both Emmanuel and Tres expressed anger toward their fathers, it was not related to their incarceration, but instead stemming from the relationship between their mother and father, something that would have existed regardless of incarceration. While it is evident from previous research, current research, and my own personal experiences that children of incarcerated parents, like most of the US population, are likely to experience ACEs at home, there also needs to be more of a strength-based focus on how families impacted by incarceration overcome obstacles to stay connected.

Families impacted by incarceration are often described as broken or torn apart and there is no doubt that incarceration is an experience that would test the most functional of families. However, during my research I did not encounter broken families. Instead, I listened to stories of families going above and beyond to remain intact. For example, even though Emmanuel's mother had remarried, she still took her sons to visit their father frequently. She also paid for phone calls so that he could remain in contact with his children and brought him packages when they visited. This was extremely important to Emmanuel. He stated:

> He always calls to check up on us. I appreciate that cuz I thought he would call once in a while but he checks up on us a lot. Like this morning I think he tried to call my phone because it said somebody is trying to call you from a correctional facility. I don't have a credit card account so I couldn't pay for it. I think my mom has to do it. It's not like you can call from a random number. You have to pay.

His mother's willingness to support the parent-child bond between Emmanuel and his father was integral to Emmanuel's father being able to maintain a relationship with his children. As Travis and Waul (2003) state, "Prisoners' success in maintaining ties with their children also often depends on the quality of their relationship with the children's caregiver" (p. 21). Amber's father also called her frequently, but she usually gave the phone to her little sister when he called. She stated:

> I don't talk to him on the phone. I just did it, like, a couple of times. I had my sister talk to him. My sister doesn't even know him. She hasn't never seen him in her life but, they have some good

conversations. Sometimes about how she's doing in school. My dad has never seen my sister, but they have the perfect conversations. It goes really well. She's like that's going to be my new dad.

Although she chooses not to interact with her dad on the phone, her statement paints the picture of a man who is a parent. He is not her sister's biological father, but still she chose him to be her new dad. There were signs that Amber was hopeful for her father's return including her recounting multiple times that he said he would show up at her doorstep one day. She also saved all of the letters and cards he sent her throughout his sentence.

Jacqueline and Orlando's family was formed in prison. Their mother's relationship with their father did not work out and eventually she began seeing a new man. Orlando remembered that his mother wanted to introduce him to her new partner and mentioned to Orlando that they would have a long wait once they arrived. He assumed that they were going to a restaurant and the wait referred to the time it would take to get a table. When they arrived at a prison he was shocked, but did not feel concerned or judgmental. Instead, he was happy to meet the man his mom "admired" so much. Jacqueline, Orlando's younger sister, also recalls being extremely excited to meet her mother's new partner. She was skeptical that he would be a good dad to her at first, but he won her over by taking an interest in her life and she loved speaking with him on the phone. She eventually began referring to him as dad and stated she felt like she could talk to him about anything. Their dad was eventually released and while the whole family was ecstatic, Jacqueline was somewhat upset that they could not spend more time together because of the requirements that reentry posed such as countless job interviews.

Vanessa also had a strong family unit that supported her through tough times. Despite being placed in foster care, Vanessa's grandmother went to court and fought for custody of her which she was eventually able to gain. She then began to live with her paternal grandparents, aunt, and cousins. Vanessa indicated that she loved spending time with her family and taking road trips, but there were still times when she missed her parents. She stated:

I want to make a system better than ACS...I feel like it would be more great for the kids [to go with their family instead of foster care] because a lot of kids grow up seeing other kids with their family and it makes them sad because they think "oh how come my parents aren't here to do this for me? I'm not good enough?"

I'm saying this because of how I think. I see my aunt be able to do things with her kids and it doesn't make me angry but I get sad because it's like I never asked for none of this...People shouldn't have to, you know what happened to me when I was younger and my grandparents had to wait to go to court and stuff like that. I feel like it shouldn't be like that because as long as they have family they should be able to go to their family.

Vanessa enjoyed a close relationship with her aunt. While her grandmother tried to force Vanessa to wear dresses and act in more stereotypically female ways, Vanessa's aunt accepted her for who she is and encouraged her to wear what makes her comfortable.

Despite the challenging situations each participant faced prior to their parent's incarceration, all of the children I interviewed, with the exception of Delilah, remained in contact with their parent and many wished they were able to have more contact. It should be noted that Delilah's decision to limit contact with her father was not directly connected to his incarceration, but instead to his substance abuse issues. Vanessa and Tres both indicated that they would like to visit their father's but the cost and distance hindered them from doing so. Research shows that this is an obstacle for many families (DeVuono-Powell et al., 2015). In 2020 the proximity bill was signed into law in New York State. This bill requires the location of an incarcerated person's children to be considered before they are placed in a facility. I experienced the impact of proximity when my father was incarcerated. The Federal Bureau of Prisons considers a person proximate to their family if they are within 500 miles which is a considerable distance (Bureau of Prisons, 2018). At times my father was in facilities over eight hours away from our home and my grandmother would spend whole weekends traveling to and from seeing my father. She also had to come out of retirement in order to help support the costs of incarceration including lawyers, visits, phone calls, and commissary. Other impediments to visiting included the overall process of visiting. This included rude correctional officers, long wait times, lack of privacy, and strict dress codes that seem to target female visitors. Tres discussed some of his issues with visiting stating:

When I used to go to the gates and stuff like that I would see mad [a lot of] prisoners who were sitting down talking to their families and people crying and it just used to be so aggravating and sad at the same time because you're going through the same thing. You feel their pain but like you don't want to hear people cry. Like you don't want to hear none of what's going on.

He describes the dehumanization during visits, not just of those incarcerated but of their families. Private moments become public. The pain of everyone is stuffed into a single room making it impossible to ignore the current circumstances. Despite this, he wished he could see his father more often.

While the discussion about the family dynamics of children of incarcerated parents prior to incarceration provides important context to the conversation about the impact of parental incarceration, there is also space to highlight the ways these families are sticking together despite the obstacles that have been placed in their way. Many families directly impacted by incarceration are not broken or torn apart, but refigured or reimagined. The level of love and strength is evident in the ways they are able to remain a family despite the criminal justice systems' best efforts to distance them.

Behavioral Impact

There have been several studies that examine the effects of parental incarceration on a child's school performance and most of them indicate some sort of correlation between parental incarceration and externalizing and internalizing behaviors. I will discuss the findings from prior research and my own research in the subsequent chapters with a focus on the behavior of children of incarcerated parents in schools. However, in this space I want to acknowledge that a growing body of literature indicates that these behaviors can be increased by the presence of unsupportive adults, especially in schools. Shalfer et al. (2019) states,

> A major issue that emerged from their work was the social challenge these children [children of incarcerated parents] experienced in regard to fears of stigmatization by teachers and peers. The researchers identified an intense internal tension between children wanting to talk about their parent's' incarceration and fear of the negative consequences of discussing it.
>
> (p. 107)

The inability to express their feelings and share their experiences in schools may exacerbate the trauma a child experiences.

Resilience

Despite many problem-based studies, there is an increasing focus on the strengths of children of incarcerated parents. Shlafer et al. (2019) states, "As researchers and practitioners, it is vital that we begin to understand how and why some children and adolescents exhibit successful adaptation, despite the considerable risks associated with parental incarceration" (p. 112). The focus on resilience should not draw attention away from the fact that parental incarceration is a traumatic event. However, there are children who have experienced parental incarceration and not only survived, but thrived. Ebony Underwood, founder of We Got Us Now, a non-profit advocacy organization led by directly impacted people, is also the child of a formerly incarcerated parent. Her father, William Underwood, spent over 30 years in federal prison before being released in 2021. His release was in no small part, assisted by Ebony and her siblings, including designer Miko Underwood, using their considerable talents to bring awareness to their father's draconian sentence. Pete Monsanto, a celebrity photographer and devoted father, also experienced parental incarceration for over 30 years. He stayed connected to his father, Pete Monsanto Sr., through a love of running. In 2019 a documentary about Pete's relationship with his father and running was released. The documentary, titled *Run for His Life*, was produced by Transform Films and provides people with an insight into the collateral consequences of mass incarceration. Yasmine Arrington, a Washington, D.C. native, is the founder of ScholarCHIPS, which assists children of incarcerated parents with mentoring, support and funds as they transition into higher education. Through her program, Yasmine has encountered dozens of children of incarcerated parents headed to college who aim to make a difference in their community. Arieanna Hollins, my niece and the inspiration for my children's book *Anna's Test* recently decided to attend Howard University in Washington, D.C., a historically Black college that most recently made headlines as the alma mater of Vice President Kamala Harris. Arieanna plans to study medicine and use her knowledge to provide quality healthcare to people in impoverished communities. While this may seem like I am bragging as a proud aunt, and perhaps that's partially true, it is also true that we rarely hear these kind of stories about children of incarcerated parents. This is not only a disservice to the research on the topic, but also to children currently experiencing parental incarceration who are receiving the message that they are more likely to end up in a jail cell than a college classroom. There are stories of success and resilience available for researchers who are willing to look for them. These stories should be normalized. There have been countless times when I have shared the story of my father's incarceration, and this, in turn, encouraged people who had never discussed the issue before to share how they too had been directly impacted by incarceration. I worked at a public-school for over a decade and enjoyed a cordial relationship with the speech and language therapist who serviced some of my students. As I became more involved in the work around parental incarceration, more people at my job became aware of my situation and my attempts to advocate not only for my students, but also for other directly impacted children. One day, in an unprovoked conversation, the speech therapist shared that she too had experienced parental incarceration during high school. I had worked with this woman for numerous years and was unaware that she and I shared this experience. Based on this encounter and the incredible network I have, I began to question how many more "successful" children of incarcerated parents exist, but remain hidden partly due to stigma, but perhaps also due to the fact that no one is searching for them. Perhaps researchers believe that a strong focus on resilience may decrease the amount of support children of incarcerated parents receive. I believe the opposite is true. Resilience is not the absence of trauma; without stress or trauma, most people would not realize how resilient they are. And while the goal is for the removal of the traumas and stressors that create resiliency, there is ample and important work that can be done around what fosters it. One of the findings these studies will most likely provide is the importance of protective factors such as healthy relationships with non-parental adults and secure economic conditions. These findings would be excellent areas to expand on practitioner and policy suggestions because they would document what is already working.

Variability

Recent research indicates that there are several variables that influence the impact of parental incarceration. No two situations are alike, even for children of incarcerated parents who live in the same household and experienced the same traumatic event. They will still experience it differently. Shlafer et al. (2019) write,

> For older children and adolescents with incarcerated parents, the role of the caregiver before a parent's incarceration, the consistency and dependability of the caregiver during the parent's incarceration, and the caregiver's psychological and tangible resources, are likely to have important implications for youths' developmental outcomes.
>
> (p. 104)

There have also been studies that indicate differences in the impact based on the race/gender of the child, gender of the parent, length of sentence, and numerous other factors (Besemer et al., 2019; Shlafer et al., 2019; Turney & Haskins, 2019). When reading any study about parental incarceration, including this one, it is important to remember that effects associated with parental incarceration are rarely caused by incarceration and instead are linked to a variety of factors. Findings on children of incarcerated parents are difficult to generalize because of these factors. Many large-scale studies lack the nuance and complexity necessary to accurately detail the experience of COIP while smaller studies, such as my own, lack the statistical relevance to be generalizable to a larger group. While there is, and will always be room for improvement, there is much to learn from the research currently available if it is read with this understanding.

Conclusion

The past decade has seen a tremendous amount of new research focused on parental incarceration and its impact on children. This has resulted in a better understanding of how children experience parental incarceration and the supports that should be provided to help assist them during this difficult time. There has also been a positive transition toward more inclusive and strength-based research. This book aims to contribute to the body of research that values the knowledge that children of incarcerated parents hold and uses their experiences and words to highlight the strengths they possess. This book will combine data from larger studies to support the findings from the original qualitative research conducted with a small group of New York City youth. In addition, my personal experiences as the child of a formerly incarcerated parent and a public-school educator will be utilized to support research and provide recommendations. I hope that with this approach, the reader will gain a more nuanced understanding of the complex lives of children of incarcerated parents. In addition, this book will be a safe space for the voices of children of incarcerated parents and their stories. While there will be numerous references to researchers throughout the book, the true experts remain those with lived experience, the children of incarcerated parents.

References

Besemer, K.L., Dennison, S.M., Bijleveld, C., & Murray, J. (2019). Effects of parental incarceration on children: Lessons from international research.

In J.M. Eddy & J. Poehlmann-Tynan (Eds.), *Handbook on children with in-carcerated parents: Research, policy and practice* (pp. 65–81). Switzerland: Springer Nature.

Breterick, D. (2019). The 'born' criminal? Lombroso and the origins of modern criminality. BBC History Extra.

Bruns, A., & Lee, H. (2019). Racial/ethnic disparities. In J.M. Eddy & J. Poehlmann-Tynan (Eds.), *Handbook on children with incarcerated parents: Research, policy and practice* (pp. 37–52). Switzerland: Springer Nature.

Bui, Q., & Miller, C.C. (2015). The typical American lives 18 miles from mom. *The New York Times*. https://www.nytimes.com/interactive/2015/12/24/upshot/24up-family.html

Bureau of Prisons. (2018). *Designations*. Retrieved from https://www.bop.gov/inmates/custody_and_care/designations.jsp

Center for Disease Control and Prevention. (2021). *Adverse childhood experiences*. National Center for Injury Prevention and Control, Division of Violence Prevention.

Christian, S. (2009). *Children of incarcerated parents*. National conference of state legislatures.

Conway, J.M., & Jones, E.T. (2015). Seven out of ten? Not even close. A review of research on the likelihood of children with incarcerated parents becoming justice-involved. Institute for Municipal and Regional Policy. Central Connecticut State University.

DeVuono-Powell, S., Schweidler, C., Walters, A., & Zohrabi, A. (2015). *Who pays? The true cost of incarceration on families*. Oakland, CA: Ella Baker Center, Forward Together, Research Action Design.

Eddy, J., & Kjellstrand, J. (2011) Parental incarceration during childhood, family context, and youth problem behavior across adolescence. *Journal of Offender Rehabilitation, 50,* 18–36.

Eddy, J.M., & Poehlmann-Tynan, J. (2019). Interdisciplinary perspectives on research and intervention with children of incarcerated parents. In J.M. Eddy & J. Poehlmann-Tynan (Eds.), *Handbook on children with incarcerated parents: Research, policy and practice* (2nd ed., pp. 3–10). Switzerland: Springer Nature.

Farrington, D.P., Murray, J., & Sekol, I. (2012). Children's antisocial behavior, mental health, drug use, and educational performance after parental incarceration: A systematic review and meta-analysis. *Psychological Bulletin, 138*(2), 175–210.

Henning, K. (2017). Boys to men: The role of policing in the socialization of black boys. In A. Davis (Ed.), *Policing the black man* (pp. 57–87). New York, NY: Pantheon Books.

International Association of Chiefs of Police. (2014). Safeguarding children of arrested parents. Bureau of Justice Assistance, U.S. Department of Justice, 1–20.

Laura, C.T. (2014). *Being bad: My baby brother and the school-to-prison pipeline*. New York, NY: Teachers College Press.

Lawrence-Lightfoot, S. & Davis J. (1997). *The art and science of portraiture.* San Francisco, CA: Jossey-Bass.

Lindsey, B. (2013). Why people keep misunderstanding the 'connection' between race and IQ. *The Atlantic.* https://www.theatlantic.com/national/archive/2013/05/why-people-keep-misunderstanding-the-connection-between-race-and-iq/275876/

Little, B. (2019). What type of criminal are you? 19th century doctors claimed to know by your face. https://www.history.com/news/born-criminal-theory-criminology

Lombroso, C. (2006). *Criminal man.* Durham, NC: Duke University Press.

Murphey, D., & Cooper, P.M. (2015). Parents behind bars: What happens to their children? *Child Trends*, 1–20.

Poehlmann, J. (2005). Children's family environments and intellectual outcomes during maternal incarceration. *Journal of Marriage and Family, 67,* 1275–1285.

Rabuy, B. & Kopf, D. (2015). Prisons of Poverty: Uncovering the Pre-Incarceration Incomes of the Imprisoned. *Prison Policy Initiative. https://www.prisonpolicy.org/reports/income.html*

Scharff Smith, P. (2019). From research to reform: Improving the experiences of the children and families of incarcerated parents in Europe. In J.M. Eddy & J. Poehlmann-Tynan (Eds.), *Handbook on children with incarcerated parents: Research, policy and practice* (pp. 267–277). Switzerland: Springer Nature.

Shlafer, R.J., Davis, L., & Dallaire, D.H. (2019). Parental incarceration during middle childhood and adolescence. In J.M. Eddy & J. Poehlmann-Tynan (Eds.), *Handbook on children with incarcerated parents: Research, policy and practice* (pp. 101–116). Switzerland: Springer Nature.

Sykes, B.L., & Petitt, B. (2019). Measuring the exposure of parents and children to incarceration. In J.M. Eddy & J. Poehlmann-Tynan (Eds.), *Handbook on children with incarcerated parents: Research, policy and practice* (pp. 11–23). Switzerland: Springer Nature.

The Sentencing Project. (2020). The Facts: Criminal Justice Facts.

Turney, K., & Haskins, A.R. (2019). Parental incarceration and children's well-being: Findings from the fragile families and child well-being study. In J.M. Eddy & J. Poehlmann- Tynan (Eds.), *Handbook on children with incarcerated parents: Research, policy and practice* (pp. 53–64). Switzerland: Springer Nature.

Travis, J., & Waul, M. (2003). *Prisoners once removed: The impact of incarceration and reentry on children, families and communities.* Washington, DC: The Urban Instituted Press.

Travis, J., & Western, B. (2017). Poverty, violence and black incarceration. In A. Davis (Ed.), *Policing the black man* (pp. 294–321). New York, NY: Pantheon Books.

2 Conducting Strength-Based Qualitative Research with Children of Incarcerated Parents

Theoretical Framework and Methods

> Make the choice to engage the community or communities that will be impacted. In short, if something is about us and supposedly for us, then it needs to be with us.
>
> (Hollins, Krupat & Underwood)

After reviewing the literature on children of incarcerated parents – which is continually growing and, in my opinion, improving – I had a clear picture of how I wanted to approach the topic. I was determined that the work I did with children of incarcerated parents would be strength-based and inclusive of those with lived experience. With Lawrence-Lightfoot and Davis (1997) in mind, I decided that I would highlight the health of children with incarcerated parents while giving space for their voices to discuss their coexisting strengths and vulnerabilities. In order to achieve this goal, I decided to conduct a qualitative study. Much of the research I read during this time (2014–2016) was based on quantitative data. While it was informative, it did not seem to capture the complexities of parental incarceration. As Siegel and Luther (2019) state:

> Qualitative research can give voice to the lived experiences of children of incarcerated parents, help us understand how children make meaning of their circumstances and provide tools to explore the complexities of the challenges faced by families of the incarcerated.
>
> (p. 149)

I wanted to provide a space for these complexities and experiences to be present and coexist. Originally, I planned to not

DOI: 10.4324/9781003202141-3

only interview youth but their caregivers and teachers. However, I eventually decided that my time would be better spent speaking with the youth participants. It was their knowledge and story that I was seeking and I wanted to know their perspective, not someone else's. I felt too many studies relied on the input of people around children of incarcerated parents as opposed to speaking with the actual children. And while speaking with caregivers and other adults can provide valuable insights, it will always be an outsider's perspective. Not even parents are 100% privy to their child's innermost thoughts and emotions. I did engage in some conversation with the caregivers, who all happened to be female, to gain background knowledge and context. However, the focus of the project remained on the lived experience and words of the directly impacted youth. To do this, I had to find a framework or frameworks that would best help me make meaning of the experiences of children of incarcerated parents. In this chapter, I will review the four frameworks I employed as a basis for exploring the experiences of these children. They are presented in order in which I believe they inform one another, beginning with critical race theory and ending with emotional labor. While I do not view any one as more important than another because they all add a unique layer of analysis and engage with one another to provide a firm foundation for understanding, I began with critical race theory because it is relevant everyone, whether they have an incarcerated parent or not. It acknowledges the way racism is ingrained in our country and informs all our social institutions. In that same vein, I wanted to forefront racism, because it is the reason the United States has so many incarcerated people and therefore it is the reason we have so many children of incarcerated parents. The critical childhood framework is the reason I wanted to speak directly to the children of incarcerated parents instead of the adults who interact with them. It views children as fully formed human beings who can make meaning of their own life and rejects the superiority of adulthood. I placed it under critical race theory, not because it was less important to this study, but because racism also informs the way people view children and childhood. Black children are often not allowed the same childhood transgressions as white children. The perception of them as children is cut short, but because they are Black they aren't granted the same privilege as white adulthood. It often just means they are viewed as a threat earlier. At first, I believed stigma would be the main theoretical framework I would be using because it was mentioned so often in studies and I assumed that it affected all children of incarcerated parents. While an understanding of stigma is undoubtedly necessary to understand the experiences

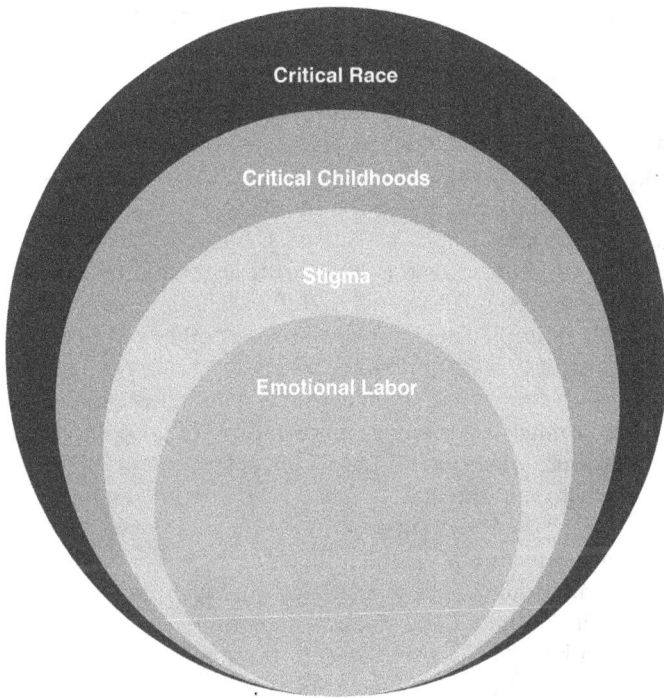

Figure 2.1 TBC.

of children of incarcerated parents, to fully appreciate their experiences including the stigma, I first had to (1) understand that stigma was compounded due to race and (2) view them as competent meaning makers who were able to convey their experiences. The final framework I explored was an adapted version of emotional labor which acknowledges the work children of incarcerated parents do to function daily because of the strong emotions and stigma that parental incarceration can present (Figure 2.1).

Critical Race Theory

I want to acknowledge in this space that not all children of incarcerated parents are children of color. However, while this book aims to provide information and support for all children of incarcerated parents, I also believe racism and its consequences are too often left out of the discussion about children of incarcerated parents. Due to the disproportionate number of Black people who are incarcerated, Black children are six times more likely to experience parental incarceration than their white counterparts (Pew Charitable Trusts, 2014). The disproportionate number of incarcerated Black people is directly related to racist policies in the United States that encourage the surveillance, arrest, and punishment Black people at higher rates than any other race in this country (Alexander, 2010; Davis, 2003). The prison boom – or the exponential increase in the number of incarcerated people – began with President Nixon's "War on Drugs." Since the war began, the number of people incarcerated for drug related offenses has increased by over 1000% (Alexander, 2010). My father was incarcerated in the 1990s multiple times for drug-related offenses. At the time, I knew nothing of this War but now I understand I was one of the casualties. Despite the façade of concern for public health, the War on Drugs had a much more sinister motivation. In 2016, former Nixon aide, John Ehrlichman, admitted to the actual intent of the War on Drugs. Ehrlichman stated:

> We knew we couldn't make it illegal to be either against the war [Vietnam] or black, but by getting the public to associate the hippies with marijuana and blacks with heroin. And then criminalizing both heavily, we could disrupt those communities. We could arrest their leaders, raid their homes, break up their meetings, and vilify them night after night on the evening news. Did we know we were lying about the drugs? Of course, we did.
>
> (LoBianco, 2016, p. 1)

Ehrlichman confirmed what many people of color had known; the War on Drugs was actually part of a continued historical war between white supremacy and Black progress. From slave patrols, to chain gangs, to the war on drugs and the invention of super predators, it is impossible to have a conversation about mass incarceration or its collateral consequences without discussing racism. Critical race theory provides a tool to examine the way racism is ingrained in the daily lives of Americans. Originally used as legal tool to expose racial discrimination, it has been adopted by many fields as a meaningful tool to analyze and challenge racism. Critical race theory consists of six tenets: (1) the permanence of racism; (2) whiteness as property; (3) the importance of counternarratives and counterstories; (4) the critique of liberalism; (5) importance of interest convergence; and (6) intersectionality (Amiot et al., 2020). These tenets are used to advance social justice and combat racism. While the criminal justice system is one of the most obvious representations of racism and racist policies, critical race theory acknowledges the role of ingrained racism in all facets of life, including schools and teaching. Children of incarcerated parents are a product of a racist system. They are overwhelming children of color. Schools are spaces that are meant to increase equity, but often do the opposite because of whiteness as property. As Hartlep (2009) writes:

> Educational policies and practices have also traditionally viewed low-income students and students of color from deficit points of view. Equally insidious, if we examine preK-12 school curricula closely, we quickly ascertain *whose* knowledge is taught, valued, and represented in schools nationwide. This hidden curriculum flagrantly services white students. At worst it demonizes students of color; at best it inconveniences them.
>
> (pp. 3–4)

This understanding is important when we address the ways schools interact with and can support children of incarcerated parents. If we begin that conversation by overlooking the obstacles they would already face in that institution due to race even without the experience of parental incarceration, we risk attributing every adverse outcome to the parental incarceration or something inherent to the child, instead of analyzing the ways in which schools underserve Black and brown students.

Another tenet of critical race theory that was particularly important to this study was the use of counterstories and counternarratives. Educators are given a space to use their voice while children are often not. Educators may negatively describe a student who doesn't turn in work or seems disengaged. When this happens, the onus is usually placed on the student or the home instead of the culture of the classroom and the teacher's interactions with their students. This study gave space for the youth, the students, to provide their side of the story. They described an environment where teachers frequently overlooked bullying and at times participated in it, seemed uninterested in challenging them and frequently gave them busy work to avoid interacting with them. In the worst case, Vanessa experienced abuse at the hands of her teacher. These are not conditions where children grow and learn regardless of whether they have an incarcerated parent or not. By sharing their counternarratives, the youth reframed the traditional focus of studies that seek to understand how parental incarceration influences adverse educational outcomes and instead challenged us to think about how schools themselves promote adverse educational outcomes for some children.

Critical Childhoods

There was an emphasis on lived experience in my study and I had to believe in the ability of the youth I was engaging with to make meaning of their own experiences and share them with me. While this may not seem like a difficult task, adults often underestimate the ability of children to understand and speak to complex matters, including their own feelings. Because I wanted to highlight the youth collaborators as experts, I utilized a critical childhood framework. Barrie Thorne (2010) explains the critical childhood perspective in her piece *Learning from Kids,* when she states:

> In my fieldwork with kids, I wanted to overcome these barriers and to approach their social worlds as ethnographers approach the world of adults; with open-ended curiosity, and with the assumption that kids are competent social actors who take an active role in shaping their daily experiences. I wanted to sustain an attitude of respectful discovery, to uncover and document kids' points of view and meanings. To adopt that basic stance means breaking with an array of common adult assumptions.
>
> (p. 408)

Thorne went on to describe the way that some adults view studying children as "studying down," much in the same way that traditional Eurocentric research viewed the study of other cultures and races. This approach places the researcher in a position of authority as if they know better than those being studied and positions them as the one giving knowledge, instead of receiving it. Because I was working with youth, particularly youth of color, I needed to employ a framework that utilized equity and rejected notions of superiority. I was there to learn from them. This was necessary because much of the previous literature spoke to the experiences of children of incarcerated parents without ever engaging with them. This, in my view, was a huge barrier to understanding the complex and unique challenges and experiences that parental incarceration presents. Providing space for the voices of children of incarcerated parents was of paramount importance to me and it was not lost on me that by doing this, I would also be providing space for the voices and counternarratives of youth of color. In order to engage in an equitable exchange with the youth, or at least as equitable as possible considering my position as an adult researcher, I had to be reflective about my own biases toward children and their competence. As Tsabary (2010) states,

> If you want to enter into a state of pure connection with [your] child, you can achieve this by setting aside any sense of superiority. By not hiding behind an egoic *image,* you will be able to engage [your] child as a *real person* like yourself.
>
> (p. 6)

Although Tsabary is discussing how a parent can better engage with their own child, I found the advice to be relevant to my study and approach as well. To engage in meaningful dialogue with youth participants, I could not view myself as superior or assume that I knew more about parental incarceration or their lives than they did. Throughout this book, I will refer to the youth I interview interchangeably as participants and collaborators. While I view participants as the more traditional academic research descriptor, at times it doesn't feel like it is enough to describe the contributions of the youth in this study. What they provided was invaluable and this book only exists because of their willingness to share their experiences. And while their names do not appear on the cover, they are just as much a part of this project as I am. They remain my collaborators in the journey to bring awareness to the experiences of children of incarcerated parents using the lived experiences of directly impacted people.

As Tsabary wrote, it was important to enter the interactions with the youth as a real person, as myself. I began the interviews by sharing who I am and what my intentions were. And while I may have been a bit more quiet than usual during our conversations to ensure that the youth collaborators had a chance to fully finish their thoughts, I remained myself. I was authentic to who I am as a person and I believe that encouraged the engaging conversations I was able to have with the participants. Authenticity was an asset. In research, there is little conversation about the authenticity of the person doing the research. Authenticity in this context could mean presenting an authentic version of yourself to the people you are seeking to study or having authentic motivations for researching a topic. Instead, there is an extreme emphasis on credentials and professional experience. While credentials and experience can be an asset when conducting research, so can authenticity. Being authentic promotes trust between the investigator and the people they seek to study. Trust allows for more intricate and vulnerable conversations. Vulnerability or being vulnerable is often used in academia in a way that evokes weakness or susceptibility. However, I am not speaking about that type of vulnerability. I am speaking to the type of vulnerability to allows us to be open and trusting of others. This is especially important in qualitative studies that seek to discuss and explore difficult topics. This type of inquiry requires the participants to be vulnerable and authentic. How can researchers expect this type of vulnerability and authenticity, if they do not model it or show up as their true selves? This is not to say the investigators should share intimate details of their lives with participants, but it does call for a level of respect, transparency and openness about their positionality and intentions. I utilized my experiences with parental incarceration to build trust with the youth collaborators. However, sharing my story was not just for that purpose. It would have felt disingenuous to show up in that space and engage in those conversations without being transparent about my own experience and why I was there in the first place. I certainly could've conducted the interviews without sharing my own story and by assuming a false outsider positioning, but I do not feel it would have yielded the same results. The conversations and insights I received were built on trust. I trusted their competence, but I also trusted them with my story. In turn, I received theirs and through this we engaged in a mutual act of healing. As Emani Davis, an adult child of a formerly incarcerated individual, once stated, for children with an incarcerated parent "healing is our revolution" (Davis, 2018, no page).

Engaging in authentic conversations with youth that assumes their competence was of vital importance to this study. It also provided an opportunity for the participants, who were all children of color and children of incarcerated parents, to provide counternarratives to narratives that present them in less than desirable ways. A critical childhood framework was vital to the way I engaged with the youth, the way we engaged in a mutual exchange of trust and the decision to forefront their voices as much as possible.

Stigma

There have been numerous studies that examine or at least mention the impact of stigma on children with incarcerated parents (Bruns & Lee, 2019; Shlafer et al., 2019; Turney & Haskins, 2019). It is commonly accepted that parental incarceration causes children to be stigmatized. What has been less acknowledged is that fact that because children of incarcerated parents are disproportionately Black and poor, they are often stigmatized because of their race, social economic status, and experience with parental incarceration simultaneously, making the impact of the stigma greater. Falk (2001) writes, "the word 'stigma' refers to the branding of slaves in ancient Greece" (p. 32). Goffman (1963) uses the same etymology, writing, "the term stigma [originated] to refer to bodily signs designed to expose something unusual and bad about the moral status of the signifier" (p. 1). While traditionally stigma was used to describe an outward sign of immorality or wickedness, it has developed into "an invisible sign of disapproval which permits insiders to draw a line around 'outsiders' in order to demarcate the limits of inclusion in any group" (Falk, 2001, p. 17). While there are some attributes that can be hidden to avoid stigma, such as sexual orientation and certain disability classifications, others are visible. While children of incarcerated parents may be able to hide their experience with parental incarceration should they so choose, they most likely cannot hide their race.

Goffman specifically wrote about the stigma surrounding incarceration and prisons. He described the families of those incarcerated as wise ones. Goffman (1963) stated:

> A second type of wise person is the individual who is related through the social structure to the stigmatized individual-a relationship that leads the wider society to treat both individuals in some respects as one. Thus the loyal spouse of a mental patient, the *daughter of the ex-con,* the parent of the cripple, the friend of the blind, the family of the hangman, are all obliged to share some of the discredit of the stigmatized person to whom they are related. One response to this fate is to embrace it, and to live within the world of one's stigmatized connexion. It should be added that persons who acquire a degree of stigma in this way can themselves have connexions who acquire a little of the disease twice-removed. The problems faced by stigmatized persons spread out in waves, but of diminishing intensity.
>
> (p. 42, emphasis added)

Children of incarcerated parents are considered wise ones. They are privy to the stigma surrounding incarceration and because of their connection to their parent, the stigma attaches itself to them as well. He notes that the most intense stigma is reserved for the stigmatized individual – in this case, the incarcerated parent. However, anyone connected to this person, including their children, receives some of the stigma as well. This understanding is important when engaging with people of color and people impacted by the criminal justice system, who are too often one in the same. Black people are often associated with criminality and incarcerated people are often perceived as violent, uneducated, and immoral. The stigma that affects children of incarcerated parents is passed through their incarcerated parent. In a sense, children of incarcerated parents are considered guilty by association.

As Shlafer et al. (2019) state "Parental incarceration can be a socially stigmatizing and isolating experience, particularly during a period of development on which peers relationships and intimacy in friendships become increasingly important" (p. 106). While discussions about children of incarcerated parents often focus on stigma and justifiably so, it is still important to remember that every child of incarcerated parents has a unique experience. For example, while many participants described being worried to a certain degree that people would judge them, not all of them did. For Amber, incarceration was such a normalized part of her and her peers' lives, that she did not worry about being judged because she was in a space with other directly impacted people. Until perceptions of incarceration change, children of incarcerated parents will most likely remain stigmatized. There are some signs that progress is being made. In 2019, FWD.us published a report that indicated that 1 in every 2 Americans has been impacted by the incarceration of a family member. As more people become "wise ones" and research continues to highlight the good in these families, the stigma surrounding incarceration may dissipate, allowing children of incarcerated parents to receive the support they deserve.

Emotional Labor

Hochschild (2003) defined emotional labor as the work a person does to "induce or suppress feeling in order to sustain the outward countenance that produces the proper state of mind in others..." (p. 7). She made a direct connection between this "work" and stigma, stating:

> My search soon led me to the works of Erving Goffman, to whom I am indebted for his keen sense of how we try to control our appearance even as we unconsciously observe rules about how we ought to appear to others. But again, something was missing. How does a person act on a feeling-or stop acting on it, or even stop feeling? I wanted to discover what it is that we act upon?
>
> (x)

While stigma may cause a person to try and control their appearance based on the rules of society, Hochschild took it a step further and explored the labor it requires to reject one's true feelings in order to please others or at least make them comfortable. Hochschild focused a lot on jobs that required social interaction, such as a store clerk or flight attendant, and the requirements to always be pleasant and smiling during the working hours despite any conflicting emotions. These kinds of workers are required to maintain a friendly demeanor despite the situation. Even if a customer is rude or offensive, the worker is expected to remain poised and pleasant despite their inner feelings. The disconnection between their outward appearance and true feelings takes an emotional toll and this is the work Hochschild writes about. While I was not engaging with workers, I was engaging with a population that for various reasons could not always present their true feelings. People of color, particularly Black people, regularly manage their emotions and reactions to avoid falling into a stereotype trap. For example, Black people are often subject to microaggressions at work. A co-worker may make an offensive comment about their hair and instead of reacting in a manner that shows anger or hurt, the Black person chooses to respond in a calm, measured tone to avoid accusations of being threatening or aggressive. The process it took to suppress their true feelings and display something else is emotional labor. Children of incarcerated parents also engage in emotional labor. They may want to share their experiences with parental incarceration with a trusted adult, but decide against it because they fear the stigma associated with incarceration. In this case, they suppress their desires in relation to stigma. Children of incarcerated parents may also engage in emotional labor at home. They may avoid sharing how hurt they are by events in their lives so they do not burden or worry their caregiver or parent. To do this, they may outwardly present as well, when inside they are struggling with a variety of emotions. Examining the ways that youth engaged in emotional labor in various settings was important to this work because it encourages people to look beyond what they see and explore the ways they can provide spaces for people of color and children of incarcerated parents to be their authentic selves.

Framework Intersections

I want to avoid framing critical race theory as important to this study solely because the participants are children of color. While it is true that children of incarcerated parents are disproportionately children of color, structural and ingrained racism affects everyone.

This understanding is important because racism isn't a Black, Latinx, Asian, or Native American issue. It is an American issue and that is inclusive of white Americans. In fact, white Americans have the greatest opportunity to eradicate racism in this country so racism cannot only be discussed among Black and brown people. No matter the race of the participants in this study, critical race theory would've remained a foundational framework because it informs the way each child experiences life. In fact, future research may want to examine the way racism and biases influence the amount of support COIP receive and how this affects ALL children of incarcerated parents, not just the ones who are people of color. A critical childhood lens was important to provide space for the voices of the youth to engage in the process of providing counternarratives which is a central tenet of critical race theory. Their counternarratives are particularly jarring when they discuss their interaction with schools. Stigma is perhaps one of the most referenced topics when it comes to children of incarcerated parents. Yet, there is space for more work that discusses how the stigma of being Black or brown interacts with the stigma of incarceration. There is also space to discuss how the perception of children as immature has often caused them to be excluded from conversations that directly affect them. Lastly, emotional labor was adapted to discuss the internal work children of color and children of incarcerated parents do to achieve a countenance that makes other people comfortable, including their caregivers and teachers.

New York City

This study was conducted in New York City, New York and all the participants were born in New York City. Most of them grew up in within the city's five boroughs, except for Amber who spent a majority of her childhood upstate due to her mother's incarceration. Delilah was not residing in New York State at the time of our interviews, but she was born and raised in the city before moving to live with an extended family member. Three out of the five boroughs of New York City are represented in the study: Manhattan, Brooklyn, and the Bronx. There were no participants who resided in Queens or Staten Island. According to the Prison Policy Initiative (2021), if New York State was a country, it would have a higher incarceration rate than the United Kingdom, Portugal, Luxembourg, and Denmark combined. The demographics of the jails and prison in New York mirror the disproportionate racial makeup of incarcerated individuals in the United States. Black people comprise 16% of New York's population, but 52% of the incarcerated population. Latinx people make up 18% of the population of New York and account for 22% of the incarcerated population. White and Asian people are both

underrepresented in New York State jails and prison (Prison Policy In-
itiative, 2021). All of the participants in the study identified as Black or
Latinx which aligns with the demographics of the jails and prisons in
New York. Due to the high number of incarcerated individuals in New
York and other factors, there has been a strong push for advocacy in
New York City and New York State. In 2020, phone calls from city jails
became free. In 2021, Governor Cuomo signed the proximity bill into law
which requires Department of Corrections and Community Supervision
(DOCCS) to consider the family of an incarcerated individual before
placement. Movements like **Close Rikers** and **Halt Solitary** have made
tremendous gains. New York City is also home to a number of non-profit
organizations meant to service people and families impacted by incarceration. We Got Us Now, Ladies of Hope Ministries, Speak Ya Truth,
Hour Children, Osborne Association, and Children of Promise all have
offices and programming in New York City. Many of the participants in
this study had a relationship with one of these organizations.

Age and Recruitment

The youth participating in this study ranged in age from 13 to 18 years
old during the time of our interviews. While critical childhood theory views all children as fully formed individuals capable of meaning-
making, this age range was chosen for practical reasons. Caregivers are
more likely to try and shield younger children from the impact of incarceration by misleading them about their parent's whereabouts. Older
children are more likely to be fully aware of their parent's incarceration and caregivers, while still protective, are more likely to trust the
youths' ability to engage in the conversation without re-experiencing
the trauma. In addition, because I was seeking detailed responses,
I thought it was best to interview children who had experienced parental incarceration for over a year and who had time to reflect on the
events of their lives. Shlafer et al. (2019) state, "older children and adolescents are capable of verbally expressing their thoughts about their
parent's incarceration. They may ask questions, express their feelings
about their parents' behaviors, or communicate their preferences
about placement and contact during a parent's incarceration" (p. 104).
I found this to be true during my interviews. The youth were able to
provide detailed and nuanced insights into not only their parent's incarceration, but also their relationships with other people and institutions such as school. Throughout the book, quotes from the following
participants are utilized to add nuance to current research. They are
presented here in order from youngest to oldest. The ages presented
are the ages they were at the time of our last interview.

- Amber is a 13-year-old biracial female residing in Manhattan. She attends a residential school in Westchester, but does not live there like some of the other students. During her mother's incarceration, Amber lived in upstate New York with her grandmother. At the time of our interview, Amber had only been residing with her mother for a year. Her younger sister also lived in the apartment. Amber also has two older brothers, both of whom are adults. One of them is incarcerated. She has been diagnosed with oppositional defiant disorder, attention deficit hyperactivity disorder and has been told that she possibly has bipolar disorder, although she is too young to be officially diagnosed. Amber's behavior when she was young caused her family to call the police and she was taken to the hospital. She said her behavior has improved and indicated that she plans to never be placed in handcuffs again. She is an expressive talker with a great sense of humor and a love of "drama."
- Jacqueline is a 13-year-old Latina who resides in Brooklyn and attends a charter school in the same borough. She is an avid cell phone user and uses it to stay connected to her extended family in Florida and Puerto Rico. She enjoys using SnapChat and engaging in streaks (consecutive days of communication) with her cousin. She describes herself as hyper and a well-known leader in her school. She doesn't have a relationship with her biological father and instead refers to her stepfather, whom she met during his incarceration, as her dad. She indicated that she was once a bully, but now uses her popularity to help other students who are having a difficult time at her school. Since the interviews, Jacqueline's dad was released and she now resides with him, her mother, and two brothers.
- Sky is a 13-year-old Black female from the Bronx who attends school in Manhattan. She dislikes going to school, but enjoys spending time with her friends. At the time of the study, her grandmother was in the hospital with cancer which caused her extreme stress. Because her father was incarcerated when she was young, she feels that she does not know him very well and can find their conversations to be awkward, but still envisions a relationship with him when he is released. Sky takes dance classes and dreams of becoming a performer one day.
- Tres is a 14-year-old Black male from the Bronx. He attends school in the Bronx and is a special education student. He was present when his father was incarcerated and remembers the day vividly. Tres was extremely excited that his father was finally able to attend one of his basketball games and on the way back to their house,

they stopped in the store. His father was apprehended in the store and Tres ran to inform his mother. Tres' relationship with his father improved during his father's incarceration. He previously disliked his father due to the way his father treated his mother. Tres was interested in basketball and his friends. He often stayed out all night, a fact that bothered his mother, but they maintained a close relationship. He considered himself the "man of the house" following his father's incarceration.

- Emmanuel is a 14-year-old Afro-Latino who resides and attends school in the Bronx. He has a deep love for his family and sports. Both of his parents were student athletes and by freshman year in high school he was well over 6-feet tall. A star athlete at his school, Emmanuel has dreams of being successful to support his mother and younger brother. He tries his best to be a father-figure to his younger brother since his father and stepfather were both incarcerated. Emmanuel's uncle died a few years ago and the lack of a male figure in his life is upsetting to him. Despite having some difficulties in school following his father's arrest, Emmanuel has become an honor roll student. He is a soft-spoken youth with a deep admiration for his mother.

- Orlando is a 14-year-old Latino who resides in Brooklyn and attends a science-based high school in the same borough. He has one younger sister, Jacqueline, and a primary school-aged brother. Orlando has a deep love for animals, both dead and alive, and nature. He enjoys playing video games and reading scientific articles to analyze their accuracy. Despite being very intelligent, Orlando dislikes traditional schooling and feels the teachers have little to offer him. He does not plan to attend college and instead would like to travel to the Dakotas to apprentice on digs in the hopes of becoming a paleontologist. He has a small group of friends who he describes as "weird." Despite being an unemotional person, he cried the day his stepfather was released from prison and surprised him at the bus stop.

- Taliyah is a 16-year-old Black female from the Bronx. She attends school in the Bronx and indicated that she "hated" her school because the people there annoy her. However, she did have a favorite teacher in school and although the teacher wasn't aware of her father's incarceration, Taliyah indicated that she would feel comfortable sharing the situation with her. Taliyah has an interest in drawing and likes to draw portraits of people. During her interview, she became visibly upset at times because she missed her dad who she described as funny or silly. Taliyah was interested in pursuing a career in criminal justice because of her father's incarceration and the reports of police brutality she saw on the news. Because the interview seemed emotionally draining for Taliyah, I only interviewed her once.

• Deliah is an 18-year-old Black female who was born in the Bronx, but resided in North Carolina with a family member at the time of our interviews. The interviews were conducted via FaceTime. Before moving out of state, Delilah was in foster care and was sexually assaulted by the son of the foster family. This coupled with both of her parent's frequent substance abuse issues caused her to have "anger issues" and engage in aggressive behavior. Delilah eventually decided to change her life and began to focus on school and getting good grades. At the time of our interviews, Delilah was in the process of obtaining her cosmetology license and hoped to open her own business. Delilah expressed more anger for her mother than her father and indicated that for her own mental health she decided to love both of her parents "from a distance." She recalled seeing her father on the street one day when she was visiting home. He was under the influence of drugs and she said they didn't speak, but instead stared at each other and cried.

• Vanessa is a 17-year-old Black female who attends a residential school in Yonkers. She remains on campus during the week, but returns home to the Bronx on weekends. After spending years in foster care, she now currently resides with her aunt and cousins. At the time of our interviews, Vanessa needed to pass one more regent exam to graduate from high school and had already created a detailed plain for her future. She plans to attend Binghamton University in upstate New York because it offers a degree in political science and is relatively close to her family in the Bronx. She plans to pay for it through a program that allows students from households under a certain income threshold to attend city or state universities for free. Following her graduation from college, Vanessa plans to join the Marines and use the benefits to attend law school. Vanessa is a very empathetic person who tries to help people on a daily basis.

All of the participants currently had an incarcerated father who had been imprisoned for over a year. Jacqueline and Orlando's father was not their biological parent and he did not reside with them prior to incarceration, but they considered him their dad. None of participants had an incarcerated mother, although three of them had previously experienced maternal incarceration. While a few of the participants had previously spent time in foster care, at the time of the interviews all of them were residing with their mother or extended family members. Two of the participants self-identified as special education students. There were also two participants who attended residential schools, but only one resided at the school part time.

Interviews

Apart from Taliyah, each participant was interviewed two or three times with each interview lasting 50–90 minutes. Seven participants were interviewed at their homes. Delilah's interviews took place via FaceTime since she was residing out of state at the time. Emmanuel's interviews took place in a location close to his home in the Bronx. Every interview was audio recorded and transcribed. The youth were asked to choose aliases for their interview. A slight majority chose to do so, with four allowing me to choose for them. The participants were informed at the beginning of our first interview about my experience with parental incarceration. At the beginning and end of each interview, participants were informed that they could request a copy of the transcript for their review. None of the participants elected to do so. They were also informed that there was a hope on my part to turn the information they provided into a book meant to increase the understanding of the experiences of children of incarcerated parents.

Exclusions

While not intentionally excluded, none of the youth I interviewed had parents who were imprisoned due to immigration policing. Children who are separated from their parents due to their parent's citizenship status are also children of incarcerated parent. The detainment of their parent can also lead to deportation, a stressor that many children of incarcerated parents do not have to contend with. As Poehlmann-Tynan et al. (2019) state:

> Research focused on the effects of parental incarceration on children and families has implications for our understanding of parent-child separations that have occurred for immigrants, including detention parents and their children. When the constant dread of arrest, detention, or deportation of parents culminates in actual family separation-whether short-lived or permanent-the results are particularly detrimental and far-reaching for children's well-being.
> (p. 349)

Working with children and families impacted by immigration policing is important work, but it can be difficult to find people willing
to participate in a study. Due to the stigma surrounding incarceration, many people are already hesitant to identify as directly impacted
individuals. Undocumented families have the additional fear of detainment and deportation, which may make them cautious when it
comes to sharing their story. I hope to read more in the future about
the imprisonment of undocumented parents and the effects it has on
their children and how that research is informed by current research
on children of incarcerated parents, but also addresses the complexities of undocumented status in the United States. I am also hopeful
that this research will be performed by a person with close ties to the
community who will use their findings to advocate for change not only
for children impacted by immigration policing, but also for children
impacted by incarceration as a whole.

Conclusion

In response to problem-based research (Shalfer et al., 2019) and an
abundance of quantitative studies (Siegel & Luther, 2019), I designed
a qualitative study that aimed to provide a more complete picture
of children of incarcerated parents and how they experience life. As
Townsend et al. (2019) state "There is more to these children than
having a parent in jail. We are working with whole people who must
be treated and considered as such" (p. 262). The theoretical frameworks used to inform the study highlight what I believe to be some
of the most important considerations when discussing the issue of
parental incarceration and its impact on children. (1) Children of incarcerated parents are disproportionately children of color and race
impacts the way they are perceived and the amount of support they
receive. (2) Children are competent actors capable of providing insight into complex subjects that affect them without the assistance
of an adult. (3) Children of incarcerated parents are impacted by the
stigma associated with criminality and incarceration. (4) Being the
child of an incarcerated parent involves a tremendous amount of
emotion and due to stigma and lack of support, children may have
to manage their emotions by themselves. While the youth collaborators had a lot in common, they were unique individuals with their
own perspectives and experiences. Conducting in-depth interviews
allowed the youth collaborators to share their stories uninterrupted.
My personal experience with incarceration set the foundation for
a safe environment. While school and education was not the main

focus of the original study, it came up often during the interviews because of the large part it played in the lives of the youth. In the next chapter, I will discuss the ways in which the collaborators described their school experience.

References

Alexander, M. (2010). *The new Jim Crow: Mass incarceration in the age of colorblindness.* New York, NY: The New Press.

Amitot, M.N., Mayer-Glenn, J., & Parker, L. (2020). Applied critical race theory: Educational leadership actions for student equity. *Race and Ethnicity Education, 23*(2), 200–222.

Bruns, A., & Lee, H. (2019) Racial/ethnic disparities In J.M. Eddy & J. Poehlmann-Tynan (Eds.), *Handbook on children with incarcerated parents: Research, policy and practice* (pp. 37–52). Switzerland: Springer Nature.

Davis, A.Y. (2003). *Are prisons obsolete?* New York, NY: Seven Stories Press.

Davis, E. (2018). *We got us now: Summer social.* New York, NY.

Falk, G. (2001). *Stigma: How we treat outsiders.* Amherst, NY: Prometheus Books.

Goffman, E. (1963). *Stigma: Notes on the management of spoiled identity.* New York, NY: Simon & Schuster Inc.

Hartlep, N.D. (2009). *Critical race theory: An examination of its past, present, and future implications.* University of Wisconsin at Milwaukee, 1–19.

Hochschild, A.R. (2003). *The managed heart: Commercialization of human feeling.* Berkeley: University of California Press.

Lawrence-Lightfoot, S., & Davis J. (1997). *The art and science of portraiture.* San Francisco, CA: Jossey-Bass.

LoBianco, T. (2016). *Report: Aide says Nixon's war on drugs targeted blacks, hippies.* CNN. Retrieved from https://www.cnn.com/2016/03/23/politics/john-ehrlichman-richard-nixon-drug-war-blacks-hippie/index.html

Luttrell, W. (Ed.) (2010). *Qualitative educational research: Readings in reflexive methodology and transformative practice.* New York, NY: Routledge.

Poehlmann-Tynan, J., Sugrue, E., Duron, J., Ciro, D., & Messex, A. (2019). Separation and detention of parents and children at the border: Lessons from the impacts of parental incarceration on children and families. In J.M. Eddy & J. Poehlmann- Tynan (Eds.), *Handbook on children with incarcerated parents: Research, policy and practice* (pp. 345–352). Switzerland: Springer Nature.

Prison Policy Initiative. (2018). New York Profile. Northampton, MA. https://www.prisonpolicy.org/profiles/NY.html

Prison Policy Initiative. (2021). United States profile. Northampton, MA. https://www.prisonpolicy.org/profiles/US.html

Shlafer, R.J., Davis, L., & Dallaire, D.H. (2019). Parental incarceration during middle childhood and adolescence. In J.M. Eddy & J. Poehlmann-Tynan

56   *Strength-Based Qualitative Research*

(Eds.), *Handbook on children with incarcerated parents: Research, policy and practice* (pp. 101–116). Switzerland: Springer Nature.

Siegel, J.A., & Luther, K. (2019). Qualitative research on children of incarcerated parents: Findings, challenges, and future directions. In J.M. Eddy & J. Poehlmann-Tynan (Eds.), *Handbook on children with incarcerated parents: Research, policy and practice* (pp. 149–163). Switzerland: Springer Nature.

The Pew Charitable Trusts, 2010. *Collateral costs: Incarcerations effect on economic mobility.* Washington, DC: The Pew Charitable Trusts.

Thorne, B. (2010). Learning from kids. In W. Luttrell (Ed.), *Qualitative educational research: Readings in reflexive methodology and transformative practice* (pp. 407–420). New York, NY: Routledge.

Townsend, T.G., Kramer, K. & Hendy, G.A. (2019). Empowering incarcerated parents of color and their families. In J.M. Eddy & J. Poehlmann- Tynan (Eds.), *Handbook on children with incarcerated parents: Research, policy and practice* (pp. 251–266). Switzerland: Springer Nature.

Tsabary, S. (2010). *The conscious parent: Transforming ourselves, empowering our children.* Vancouver, CA: Namaste Publishing.

Turney, K., & Haskins, A.R. (2019). Parental incarceration and children's well-being: Findings from the fragile families and child well-being study. In J.M. Eddy & J. Poehlmann- Tynan (Eds.), *Handbook on children with incarcerated parents: Research, policy and practice* (pp. 53–64). Switzerland: Springer Nature.

3 Children of Incarcerated Parents in Schools

Their Perspectives and Interaction with the Education System

> I got bullied a lot in middle school, high school and elementary. I wasn't that fortunate, the clothes I wore – I got bullied about that. I didn't have people to help me after school with my homework so I got teased because I'd always ask people at school to help me. The teachers would just yell at me and I would get in trouble. I never tried to tell them.
>
> (Vanessa)

Schools are one of the most important institutions in our society. Ideally, schools are safe spaces where children can happily grow and learn. When parents send their children to school, they are hopeful that their child is being tenderly cared for while simultaneously learning the skills necessary to be successful in society. We hope that our children learn not only how to read, write, and solve mathematical equations, but also how to make and maintain friends and respect other people. These are high expectations, but understandable considering the propaganda that surrounds schools and schooling.

While our country is politically divided, one platform candidates from all political parties seem to highlight is their support for education. Schools have been touted as the great equalizer. In fact, there is a law that states all children in the United States are entitled to a free, public education. Many people use schools and education to uphold the so-called meritocracy in the United States. The idea of meritocracy is simple; that everyone is afforded the same opportunities and with intelligence, skill, and determination, a person can completely change their circumstances and achieve the American dream. In a meritocracy, a child born into poverty in rural Arkansas has the same chance for success as the offspring of a wealthy investment banker living in Manhattan. It sounds lovely. In a meritocracy, race, class,

DOI: 10.4324/9781003202141-4

gender identity, sexual orientation, disability status, citizenship status, or even physical appearance do not factor in to one's ability to meet society's definition of success – which is often linked to your salary and job title. Instead, it seems as if everyone, no matter where they are from or who they are, is given the one gift they need to get ahead; education. Since everyone is provided with an education, one's success or lack thereof is not the result of societal ills such as systemic racism and discrimination, but instead it becomes the decision of the individual. If a person is not successful in school or in life, it is seen as a personal failing; a failing of the child, the parents, and often the community.

This type of thinking allows many people, including educators, to further marginalize and oppress certain groups of children. Mark (2020) states:

> Meritocracy is a false and not very salutary belief. As with any ideology, part of its draw is that it justifies the *status quo* (emphasis in original), explaining why people belong where they happen to be in the social order. It is a well-established psychological principle that people prefer to believe that the world is just.
>
> (p. 1)

While Mark's observation that people want to believe the world is "just" is interesting, I'd argue that many people, especially people of color, already know the world is not just and with each passing day, that becomes more and more clear to those who are willing to see it. For many who are anxiously awaiting the verdict for the case against Derek Chauvin, the police officer who knelt on George Floyd's neck for over nine minutes as people recorded the life leaving his body, they know the verdict won't be "just." Even if Chauvin is convicted, which is still uncertain despite video evidence and multiple eye witnesses, many would not describe that as just or justice. It would instead be some sort of accountability for the police officer who seemed confident in his right to murder a Black man in broad daylight. Justice, defined as righteousness, equitableness, or moral rightness, would be if all people were treated equitably and fairly. If justice were truly served, there would be no need for a trial because George Floyd would still be with us. Being a tall Black man would not be viewed as a threat. His daughter, Gianna, would have a father instead of a cause. His daughter has been posted across social media with a sign that says *Daddy Changed the World*, but if given the option, I'm sure Gianna would give the world to have her father back. Wanting or choosing to believe the world is just may be a "well-established psychological principle," but the ability to do so fully is rooted in privilege. Many people, especially people of color, try to be optimistic that the world has the potential to become just while dealing with daily experiences that prove just how unfair it truly is. Instead, I believe the most important part of the statement is how meritocracy "justifies the *status quo*." What is the status quo in the United States? While this may receive a wide-range of responses depending on who you ask, my stance is that the status quo in the United States is the acceptance of white supremacy and systemic racism as a normal part of life. In the 244 years since the United States formed and elected its first president, only one of them has been a person of color. This did not occur until 2008, when Barack Hussein Obama was elected. I chose to use his full name here because it has often been used in a malicious way to signal otherness. It is a strong name with African roots, but now will always be representative of America. Obama was number 44 out of 46 presidents and his successors have both been white males. His election was touted as the sign of a post racial society, but the status quo remains. In this country, progress or even the façade of progress, is too often met with a strong push back. Kamala Harris smashed the glass ceiling in 2020, becoming the first Black and South Asian female vice president in our history. It was a victory and perhaps a chip in the status quo, but still it remains. Congress, the governing body meant to reflect the thoughts, feelings, and wishes of its representative population, is proof of this. Schaeffer (2021) writes:

> Although recent Congresses have continued to set new highs for racial and ethnic diversity, they have still been disproportionately White when compared with the overall U.S. population. Non-Hispanic White Americans account for 77% of voting members in the new Congress, considerably larger than their 60% share of the U.S. population overall. This gap hasn't narrowed with time: In 1981, 94% of members of Congress were White, compared with 80% of the U.S. population.
>
> (p. 1)

In the United States, white people, particularly white males, hold a disproportionate amount of powerful positions, including those in our governing bodies. To believe in meritocracy in the United States, is to believe in the superiority of the white race. Yes, personal qualities are important, but if personal qualities and access to education are all that one needs to be successful, one must examine and explain why white people are in so many positions of power. Since everyone presumably has access to a free education, are we then to believe that white men simply have superior qualities that merit their positions while other races and genders do not? While many may not think about meritocracy in these terms, it is important to examine what it actually implies and the damage promoting it can do, especially in schools.

Similar to the demographics of Congress, the teaching profession is majority white, although in contrast to Congress, it is also a majority female. According to the National Center for Education Statistics (2020), during the 2017–2018 school year, 79% of public-school teachers were white and 76% were female. Black teachers made up just 7% of all public-school teachers; a 1% decrease from the prior decade. Nine percent of public-school teachers identified as Hispanic (this was considered a separate identity from Black or white) and 3% identified as Asian or Native American. These numbers are mirrored when looking at the demographics of principals, with 78% identifying as white during the same period. These figures are particularly interesting as we look at the demographics of public-school students in the United States. A 2018 ACLU report found that for the first time in American history, white students are now the minority in public schools. Other groups including students who identify as Black, Hispanic/Latino (any race), Asian, Native American, Multi-Racial, or Pacific Islander now account for 51% of the public-school population. The teachers and administration in schools are often not reflective of the student body. This is not to say that white teachers are incapable of teaching children of color or that being of the same race as your students automatically makes someone a superior teacher. That argument is not being made here. However, white teachers benefit from white privilege and while that is not something they can change, they do have a choice as to how to handle their privilege. The first step is admitting this, however that is not an easy task, even though it seems as if it should be. Richard Carranza, the former chancellor of the New York City Department of Education, the largest school system in the country, encountered an intense backlash over the implementation of implicit bias trainings in schools. The backlash included former high-ranking administrators suing Carranza and the DOE over claims that they were demoted due to their "whiteness." The backlash was not limited to high-ranking employees. While many teachers felt that implicit bias training was long overdue, there were others who described it as toxic and anti-white. While other reasons have been given for Chancellor Carranza's departure, one cannot help but think that his clash with whiteness and white supremacy, something many inaccurately think does not exist in New York, was simply too much to handle. With or without Carranza, the tensions remain. In 2021, the Educational Researcher published a study that described the difficulty retaining Black teachers in the public-school system. The study found that although some Black teachers (10%) cited personal factors such as age, salary, and sex as reasons for thinking of leaving teaching, almost double (17%) cited experiences of microaggressions as their reason for possibly leaving. Terada (2021) states:

> Black teachers often feel that their contributions aren't acknowledged, their competence is unfairly questioned, or their assertiveness is perceived as aggression or anger. Ultimately, experiencing microaggressions on a regular basis can make teachers feel like second-class citizens in the school community.
>
> (p. 1)

This study validated my personal experiences in the public-school system. Despite completing my PhD, my ideas were often dismissed or ignored, even when I felt they directly benefited the children. At one point, I offered to facilitate a support group for children directly impacted by mass incarceration at my school. To avoid potential obstacles, I worked out a schedule that allowed for me to host the group during my lunch or preparatory period. I also offered to speak at the PTA meeting to share my personal experience and credentials, including the fact that I co-authored the curriculum and it had already been piloted at another school. I was gently informed by administration that implementing this type of curriculum could give the impression that we view the parents at my school in a certain way. Hopeful, I explained the reach of mass incarceration and highlighted that fact that almost any school in America could implement this program. I emailed a sample permission slip for review and left the office feeling optimistic the children's best interests would outweigh adult discomforts. My email was never returned. I could not help but feel that not only was my expertise being questioned, but that the interest of adults, in this case the principal, was being placed above that of the children. A year later I found myself feeling stifled again as the George Floyd murder entered the discussion among my colleagues. There was a meeting meant to calm tensions among the staff, who became embroiled in an argument when a Black employee posted a meme which declared that people who are silent have chosen the side of the oppressors. I took no offense and agreed that as a school that services a predominately Black population, we needed to speak more about what was occurring. However, some staff, particularly a few white females, were offended. The ensuing meeting consisted of the white female principal crying as the staff, myself included, descended into chaos. At one point a white colleague cried as she described the challenges she faced because she had to speak to her daughter about white privilege. Admittedly by this point I had lost my patience. I was a Black woman with a Black son who was tired of centering white comfortableness over Black grief. I responded that explaining white privilege to a white child is not the same as explaining racism to a Black child. In fact, I considered it a privilege that her child had made it to her teenage years without ever having the conversation, while conversations with my son about his racial identity began at age four. She cried and said I did not know if her daughter would ever experience racism because she might "marry a Black man." This statement bothered me for several reasons. Being a biracial Black woman, my mother, despite having Black children and a Black husband, enjoys a white privilege that I may have benefited from at times, but will never fully experience. My mother has been privy to the racism her husband and children encounter, but she is always adjacent to the racism, never the target. Also, proximity to Blackness is not the same as being a part of or an ally to the Black struggle. Making a hypothetical Black husband for her teenage child did not make her or her daughter incapable of racism. In fact, during that exchange I felt she displayed the opposite. However, I still found myself lacking allies with the exception of one like-minded colleague. Most people remained silent, although I did receive some texts messages from a few of my colleagues who were supposedly shocked by the exchange. I was not shocked. I worked in that particular school for over a decade and heard microaggressions toward students and faculty on a consistent basis. Teachers referring to Black students as animals or gorillas. White teachers pretending to compliment a Black teacher's hair. *I wish I didn't have to brush my hair to come to work.* The refusal of certain staff members to participate in a Black History Month show that featured a tribute to victims of police brutality because it was "anti-police." The white assistant principal calling a young Black male "boy" when he was angry. These are just a few of the innumerable incidents of anti-Black behavior that was a part of the culture in the building. As a person of color in that environment, I felt helpless. I wanted to stay to help the children, but I feared becoming complicit in the system. I felt like I was constantly under attack for trying to work toward an equitable school environment. By the end, I was actually under attack. In addition to being told by one of my white colleagues that I am constantly complaining, my union representative informed me that some of my white colleagues felt unsafe and threatened. At first, I was not sure how I was threatening, especially since the meeting took place over a virtual conferencing platform, but then I realized being Black is enough to be a threat to some people. Being Black and using your voice is enough to be viewed as downright dangerous. What people found threatening was a Black woman calling out white supremacy in a predominately white space. In the end, I decided my mental health was more important than remaining at that job, but I still often think about the children left behind to be indoctrinated in a culture of white supremacy because some teachers do not see their humanity. If this is how some of the staff treats adults of color in the building, imagine how they treat the children.

While some may view meritocracy and racism within school buildings as separate from the experience of children of incarcerated parents in schools, they are intersecting issues. While all children of incarcerated parents are not children of color, the disproportionality within US jails and prisons means that children of incarcerated parents are also disproportionately children of color. Meritocracy and the perpetuation of the status quo directly impact the experiences of children in schools, especially children of color and children of incarcerated parents. As Lyiscott (2019) states, "...our systems of education are often force-fed to us as politically and ideologically neutral spaces that seek to propel anyone forward if only they would 'pull themselves up by their bootstraps.' These lies are nothing short of gaslighting..." (p. 70). In schools, meritocracy is the costume that racism wears to appear less offensive and allow the user to oppress without reflection. This presents itself in many ways. There have been numerous studies that have documented school performance indicators and compared them across race, class, gender, and other identifiers. The usual outcome is that in general, white children perform better than their peers of color, with the exception of Asian students (Darling-Hammond, 1998; Institute of Educational Sciences, 2019; Spector, 2019). The explanation for this phenomenon depends on the study and can range from the so-called cultural deficits of Black and Latinx families to lack of funding or resources in certain communities. For example, Lyiscott (2019) states,

> Because the United States is pretty much as segregated now as it has ever been, glaring statistics that reflect this segregation mark P-16 institutions across the nation, myriad educational inequities emerge out of the racial and economic disparities that cause P-12 schools in lower and working-class communities of color to be severely under-resourced and structurally stagnated.
>
> (p. 70)

One perspective that I find especially relevant is that schools in the United States were built and intended to service white males. The first school in the 13 colonies was the Boston Latin School, which was established at a time when Black children were considered property. In the following century, several states passed laws that made it illegal for enslaved Black people to read or write. When schools did become open to different races, they were segregated, underfunded and inequitable. This should not up for debate as the Supreme Court acknowledged the differences between segregated schools in the landmark *Brown v. Board of Education* case. The ruling in this case was more of a legal landmark than an actual catalyst for real change. There is a saying in criminal justice circles that the criminal justice system is not broken, it is operating exactly the way it was designed. This means that the discrimination found in the criminal justice is not coincidental, but intentional. The same can be said about the school system. It is not broken. It is working how it was designed. Our schools value and uplift white culture, while encouraging children of color to assimilate to white middle class ideals. American schooling believes in the potential and promise of white children; it tolerates students of color. Some may read this and question the validity of the statement. They may point to a kind teacher or school they attended or taught at that was particularly progressive to refute this assertion. The presence of kind teachers or progressive schools is important, but they alone cannot reform an inherently inequitable system and using them as a way to undermine social justice is counterproductive. As Delpit (2012) states:

> The problem is that the cultural framework of our country has, almost since its inception, dictated that "black" is bad and less than and in all arenas "white" is good and superior. This perspective is so ingrained and normalized that we all stumble through our days with eyes closed to avoid seeing it. We miss the pain in our children's eyes when they have internalized the societal belief that they are dumb, unmotivated, and dispensable.
>
> (p. xviii)

The oppression of children of color in schools is not just seen in test scores or other performance indicators. It can be seen in attendance and suspension rates as well. The ACLU (2019) found that Black children lost nearly five times the amount of instructional days than their white peers due to disciplinary measures each school year. Students with disabilities were twice as likely as their able-bodied peers to be suspended. Being suspended from school has been linked to a variety of negative outcomes. As Flannery (2015) asserts, "A suspension can be life altering. It is the number-one predictor-more than poverty-of whether children will drop out of school, and walk down a road that includes greater likelihood of unemployment, reliance on social-welfare programs and imprisonment" (p. 42). The transition from school system to criminal justice system is well-written about. Some researchers refer to it as the school-to-prison pipeline, while others have expanded on the concept and refer to it as the cradle-to-prison pipeline (Laura, 2014) or the Universal Carceral Apparatus (Shedd, 2015). These terms all refer to certain systems and procedures that people encounter, often from a young age, that make it more likely for them to become justice involved, including the presence of police in schools. The presence of school resources officers (SROs) increased in the 1990s following several school shootings. While these officers are supposedly there to protect students, the presence of police in schools has led to the increased surveillance and criminalization of Black and brown youth. Henning (2017) writes:

> Ironically, SROs (school resource officers) are especially common in impoverished communities, notwithstanding evidence that most recent mass shootings have occurred in schools and other venues dominated by middle-class whites...As expected, school-based arrests disproportionately affect black boys and contribute significantly to the "school-to-prison-pipeline." Studies show that schools with higher percentages of black and Hispanic students are more likely to employ school resource officers or other security personnel.
>
> (pp. 66, 67)

SROs are quite common in New York City where the youth collaborators in my study attend school. Many New York City youth are familiar with the process of going through a metal detector and being patted down before being able to enter the school building. Offenses such as fighting or disorderly conduct that used to warrant a trip to the principal's office and school-based consequences could now lead to arrest when police are present in schools. This is not just true of high school students. In 2019, a six-year-old student in Florida was placed in zip-tie handcuffs by officers after she allegedly hit three staff members. She screamed "Help me! Help me!" as the police walked her out and into the police car. A staff member questioned the police as to if the restraints were necessary and the officer responded in the affirmatory, stating that if the girl were any larger she would've been "wearing regular cuffs." The six-year-old, who is Black, was charged with battery and the charges were later dropped. Throughout this country, students as young as Kindergarten are being introduced to the criminal justice system at school. This type of trauma at an early age, especially instigated in a school setting and by school staff, shows how far we are from the ideal of schools and schooling for many of our students. Children of incarcerated parents, who are often Black, brown, and poor, are already entering an institution that may dehumanize them because of their race and/or socio-economic status. They are then disadvantaged again by the stigma and stereotypes that surround incarceration. If students reveal to the school and their teachers that they have a parent in prison, studies have shown that teachers are more likely to have a negative perception of the student (Ciccone et al., 2010). If they keep their parent's incarceration to themselves, they will not receive any support from the teachers or the school. Although given the current level of support for children of incarcerated parents in schools, even if they did share their situation with a teacher, there would not likely be any school-based support available outside of the guidance counselor anyway. Even access to the guidance counselor would be dependent upon the school's staffing. A 2019 ACLU report found:

- 1.7 million students are in schools with police but no counselors.
- 3 million students are in schools with police but no nurses.
- 6 million students are in schools with police but no school psychologists.
- 10 million students are in schools with police but no social workers.
- 14 million students are in schools with police but no counselor, nurse, psychologist, or social worker.

(p. 4)

Given the ways in which schools often fail to support the most marginalized children and instead enact methods of oppression themselves, I am going to explore the school-based experiences of some of the youth collaborators from my study and how their experiences live at the intersection of race and the collateral consequences of mass incarceration.

I want to examine the story of a teen who lived in the Bronx and identified as a Black female. For my study, she chose to use the alias *Vanessa*. During the time Vanessa spoke with me, she was enrolled in high school and living with her paternal aunt. She was one of four siblings, but none of her brothers or sisters lived with her and they had not lived together for quite some time. The reason for their separation was their father's incarceration for substance abuse and their mother's struggle with the same issue. The separation of her family was something that affected Vanessa profoundly. While discussing her family, Vanessa stated,

> it doesn't make me angry but I get sad because it's like I never asked for none of this but if I could all I would want to ask for is a family. I would want to see my sister every day when I wake up. I would want to be able to be with them and hang out with them but I can't.

Due to her parent's issues with substance abuse, Vanessa entered the foster care system around age four. Initially, she was placed with her older sister and both were exposed to horrendous abuse at the hands of their foster parents. Vanessa remembers being physically and verbally abused. She also recalled that her sister was sexually abused. Despite these difficult circumstances, Vanessa was still expected to attend school. As an educator, I was hopeful that school provided a haven for Vanessa during the day, but what she described was quite the opposite. Vanessa was bullied by her peers and yelled at by her teachers for issues beyond her control. When I inquired if her teachers were understanding about her incomplete homework assignments, Vanessa indicated that they would just yell at her and she would get into trouble. While this is troubling, Vanessa's story especially as it relates to education, continues down an upsetting path. Separated from her parents and some of her siblings, Vanessa continued to be abused in her foster home and teased at school. Eventually her sorrow and pain began to present itself as anger and she started getting in trouble at school. She was given a classification and placed in a special education classroom. She was also prescribed medication meant to calm her behavior and improve her school performance. However, Vanessa indicated that the medication made her tired and caused her to gain weight which led to more bullying. When she was in middle school, her psychiatrist suggested to her family that Vanessa might have more success in a residential school. The psychiatrist told the family that if Vanessa was placed in a residential school, the dosage of Vanessa's medication could be lowered. Vanessa spoke about her initial trip to the school and how she adjusted during our conversations. She stated:

> I was 12 years old. I didn't know I was going. I was tricked. I was told I was going to a Boston Red Sox game. I was 12 years old. My sister had moved. My brother was adopted. My other brother

was living with his father. Maybe it was the best thing for me at the time. Maybe it wasn't. I was getting bullied at the time and moving to another state really wasn't the best thing. So, I went there. I got bullied there. They started reducing my medication. My medication made me out of it. I was sleeping all the time. I was dozing off all the time. I was always hungry. I always had to use the bathroom because of it. They reduced it and then they cut it. One day one of the kids there tried to pick on me and I actually spoke up and they were surprised. There was so many kids that were corrupted in one environment that either you're going to do it [misbehave] or get picked on so I didn't want to get picked on so I did bad. I was always still good in my academics, but I became aggressive. I got restrained a lot, sometimes like 4 or 5 times a day. Then it got to the point where I started doing really good, like really, really good and I didn't want to do bad anymore because I wanted to leave. I would earn rewards and stuff like that and I could go home on home visits.

Despite reporting that she was engaged in numerous altercations during her time at the school, Vanessa eventually realized that the only way to leave the school was to follow the school rules and advance to the highest level. The school had a tiered system that granted more freedom and privileges each time a student leveled up. However, her intentions to do better did not go unchallenged. One of most disturbing incidents Vanessa shared with me happened on a school bus. She shared the following:

I was on the bus and I went to say good morning to one of the little boys. He was seven. He was the youngest kid on the bus and so I went to give him a high five and he's autistic and there's another boy that's like 10 years old and he envied the other boy and he went to grab my headphones and I grabbed my headphones back and he started hitting me. So, I'm letting this little boy hit me and the staff ain't doing anything so I smacked him. And the staff got up and pushes me and they push me around and they have me in a lock. I was trying to get out so I pushed myself to the ground and the staff fell on top of me- it's a male staff on top of that and he has kids and he's doing this to someone else's kid. So, he falls on top of me and I'm trying to get up and he's pushing his knee on me so I can't get up. He's in the corner kneeing me so I get up and I kicked him. I was so disgusted with myself after. I got so angry I spit on him and I was disgusted because spitting is a really nasty thing to do, but I was so angry. My aunt and my grandmother came up to see me and they reviewed the cameras and my aunt was asking questions and it wasn't adding up so eventually I got discharged. But like while I was there the staff was very physical and aggressive. I had a black eye a few times- I still have pictures if you want to see. My arm was broken a few times from the staff and restraints. They would say oh she's biting me which I would never do and the proper thing is to push your elbow into their mouth because you aren't feeling the pain, they [the person attempting to bite] are in their jaw, but he would say "she's biting me" and throw his elbow into my eye. Each time I felt it. He kept saying she's biting me. "Bite release! Bite release!"

It was difficult to listen to Vanessa's story because it seemed as if almost every adult in her life failed her at some point, including her teachers. When discussing children in foster care, the US Department of Education (2020) states, "A positive PK-12 education experience has the potential to be a powerful counterweight to the abuse, neglect, separation, impermanence and other barriers these vulnerable students experience" (p. 1). However, early in her school career, Vanessa was struggling to complete her homework assignments and was experiencing bullying from her peers. Instead of supporting her, Vanessa's teachers increased her pain and isolation by yelling at her about something that was out of her control. Due to the behavior of her teachers, Vanessa never confided in them about her parent's incarceration or the abuse she was experiencing in her foster home. Instead, she withdrew and eventually was placed in the residential home where she suffered more abuse. After suffering multiple injuries at the hands at staff members, Vanessa's aunt, and grandmother, with whom she would then reside, came to retrieve her. Far from being a sanctuary, most of Vanessa's experiences with schooling were nightmarish. Although Vanessa's story may seem like an anomaly, it is probably more common than people would like to admit. Per the National Resource Center on Children and Families of the Incarcerated, 15%–20% of children entering the child welfare system have an incarcerated parent (2014, p. 1). Once in foster care, a child is more likely to be placed in special education. The Legal Center for Foster Care and Education (2018) found that school-aged children in foster care are 2.5–3.5 times more likely to receive special education services than their peers (p. 7). There have also been numerous reports of abuse at residential schools. Historically, some may be familiar with the atrocities committed at residential schools in the 19th and early 20th centuries devoted to "civilizing"

Native Americans. Describing that experience, Pember (2019) whose mother attended one such school writes:

> This is what achieving civilization looked like in practice: Students were stripped of all things associated with Native life. Their long hair, a source of pride for many Native peoples, was cut short, usually into identical bowl haircuts. They exchanged traditional clothing for uniforms, and embarked on a life influenced by strict military-style regimentation. Students were physically punished for speaking their Native languages. Contact with family and community members was discouraged or forbidden altogether. Survivors have described a culture of pervasive physical and sexual abuse at the schools. Food and medical attention were often scarce; many students died. Their parents sometimes learned of their death only after they had been buried in school cemeteries, some of which were unmarked.
>
> (p. 1)

More recently, in a world that was culturally very different from Pember's family, Paris Hilton described her experience with abuse at a Utah boarding school. Similar to Vanessa's experience, this boarding school was supposed to support youth with challenging behaviors and employed a level system. Like Vanessa, former students of the school indicated consistent abuse from the staff. Miller (2020) states,

> They [former students] spoke of repeated physical restraints, with up to 10 staffers piling on young children. Some were chemically sedated, or so overmedicated they felt like a zombie. Others spoke of being left in isolation rooms for days after getting in trouble for things like not getting out of bed or asking for an inhaler.
>
> (p. 1)

The use of physical force, severe punishment for minor infractions, and use of medication as a means of control were present in the residential schools in the 19th century and persist today. This is not to say that ALL residential schools and staff abuse children, but it does highlight that society's solution to children with undesirable behaviors, and it should be noted that undesirable behaviors are sometimes just behaviors outside of traditional white middle class values, is to simply send them away. Unfortunately, many of those children's challenging behaviors began because of a lack of adult support and understanding and sending them away only intensifies their distrust of adults and institutions. If millionaire Paris Hilton can be sent away and abused, what does that mean for the children without her white privilege or financial means? Paris Hilton was able to describe her horrific abuse to a state Senate committee; Vanessa only has this book.

While not all of the youth I interviewed had an educational experience like Vanessa, most did not view school as a positive space for a variety of reasons. One of the main reasons was the prevalence of bullying, which almost each collaborator I spoke with described in some detail. According to the National Center for Education Statistics (2020), 20% of students aged 12–17 reported being bullied at school in 2017. However, it would be a mistake to view bullying as an issue that only affects the child being bullied. Pervasive bullying affects the culture of a building and forces students into certain roles; the bullied, the bully, the bystander or the defender. Youth may switch from one role to another depending on the context or embody more than one role at a time. A defender might easily become the bullied. The bullied may become a bully. A bully may also be bullied in certain spaces. Nonetheless, the fear of being bullied is present in schools. Vanessa detailed being bullied by other students due to her clothes and lack of parental support. Tres, a 14-year-old Black male from the Bronx, also remembered being bullied in school. However, he indicated that once his physical presence began to increase, the bullying ceased. Ironically, this growth that protected him school, also made him a target in other spaces. Tres recalled visiting his father in prison and the feeling of uneasiness as the guards interacted with him. He stated:

> When I was first there [on a visit] I didn't like it because the security guards just look at me for some reason. I was tall for a little kid. When I used to come they would think I was older and I was young. I used to feel like they were picking on me. Like the way they were staring at me because of my skin, I don't know. I'm not racist, but I don't know just the way they was talking to me seemed like they was trying to be threatening or something. And then I was just not paying attention to it because it's a prison and I just wanted to see my pops.

Tres went from being bullied in school to being bullied by the staff when he visited his father. Because of his stature, Tres felt the guards viewed him as a threat. While Tres story was anecdotal, it is impossible not to view it in a larger context. There have been numerous publications about the adultification of Black and brown children (Burton, 2007; Henning, 2018; Laura, 2014; Morris, 2019). However, one does not need to be an academic to watch it play out in real life. Thirteen-year-old Adam Toledo, a Latino, was recently gunned down by an officer employed by the Chicago Police Department. As newsrooms covered the story, many were paying attention to the coverage the story received. Sean Hannity, a Fox News political commentator known for his conservative views and thinly veiled (often naked) racism, referred to Adam as a 13-year-old man. This was a stark contrast to Hannity's comments of Kyle Rittenhouse, a 17-year-old who traveled across state lines armed with a rifle and ended up murdering two protestors. Hannity, during his coverage of those events, referred to Rittenhouse, a white male, as a boy. Why is Toledo a man and Rittenhouse a boy despite the latter being four years older? Race. From Trayvon Martin to Tamir Rice, Black bodies are viewed as threats from an early age in this country. Tres felt that when the guards sized him up. Although he was no longer being pushed around at school, he recognized that he now had a new, more dangerous adversary; white supremacy. There were other incidents of bullying mentioned throughout the collaborators' interviews. Jacqueline, a 14-year-old from Brooklyn said she was once a bully herself when she was angry from issues at home. She has since changed her ways and tries to use her popularity to help others navigate the school social rules. She stated:

> There's a lot of bullying in my school and so my school now has this thing where we have bullying sessions every week and me, personally, I don't get bullied. Like I admit that I was a bully once 'cause of the things that was happening at home and I admit that I wasn't the nicest person I could be to other people, but now I'm like helping this one girl out. She's getting bullied a lot at my school 'cause she has like a growing disorder and so she's really short and so I like I help her out with whatever I can do to help her and like give her friends and stuff 'cause I don't want to sound popular in my school, but I'm known and I feel like if I introduce her to some of my friends then she'll have like a lot more friends.

Her brother, Orlando, was less interested in the politics of the school social order and preferred to maintain close ties with a small group of friends and spend his free time playing video games or studying animals. Still he was not immune to bullying in school. However, he was comfortable in his role as bystander. He did not bully others, but avoided intervening when others were being bullied so he did not become a victim himself. One of the things I found most interesting about the collaborators discussions around bullying were that they never mentioned being bullied or others bullying someone because their parent was in prison. Vanessa was bullied for issues stemming from her parent's substance abuse and incarceration (lack of financial means, lack of home support), but it was never explicitly about incarceration. This is an important distinction to make. When people speak about children of incarcerated parents and bullying, it is often in the context that the children are being bullied about their parent's incarceration. This places the onus of blame on the parent and adds to the perception that the difficulties children face when their parents are incarcerated are ultimately the fault of parent. If the parent is at fault, it is easy to look beyond the responsibility of the school. However, these children were not bullied because their parent was incarcerated; they were bullied because it was a part of the school culture. This is detrimental to all students whether they are the bullied, bully, bystander or defender. Schools need to take a proactive approach to lessening the amount of bullying happening within their walls. In addition, when we speak out children of incarcerated parents and bullying, we need to be mindful to frame the conversation in a way that doesn't blame parents or families, but instead highlights the negative impact the stress of bullying can cause all children, but especially children of incarcerated parents who are already dealing with the strain of parental incarceration. When the conversation is framed in this way, it allows people to explore what schools and school staff can do to better support all children, including students who may be dealing with additional trauma, such as children of incarcerated parents.

In addition to bullying, another major area of concern was the relationship between teachers and children of incarcerated parents. There were numerous incidents throughout the interviews, where my collaborators expressed that their teachers seemed to have lowered expectations or lacked concern for their academic progress. Amber, a 15-year-old female from Manhattan, attended a residential school, but did not reside on campus. She had aspirations of going to college and obtaining a job that paid a high salary because she believed that "money is like life; you can't do anything if you don't have money." However, despite her aspirations, Amber felt unchallenged in her school setting and spent most of her time walking the halls with the acceptance of the school staff. She stated:

> Unless I'm being bribed to do something good and stay in class I'm not there. If I'm being bribed I'm not going to leave. I'm going to be in school, but I'm bribed a lot. It's boring, and I know most of the stuff that they're teaching me. And, most of my classes are

in gym right now. I have like three gyms and then three maths. Then, I have lunch period and then one English. People say I have a pretty fun schedule. I don't like gym. I like the halls. I don't know why I don't get credit for walking around the halls.

Amber felt little motivation to be in class because she found it to be boring and unengaging. Her assertion that she already knew the material explained why she may feel this way. Because she was attending a residential school, it is possible that the curriculum was remedial and the teachers were more focused on behavior management than content. However, part of great classroom management is student engagement. Because Amber was not challenged, she needed external motivators to attend class. It makes sense. If the purpose of school is to learn, why attend class when you already know the content? Some may answer because those are the rules, but pedagogical strategies tell educators to avoid telling children to do things without a sound backing. Best practices in teaching encourages educators to use multiple means of engagement to include all learners in the lesson. Amber seemed confident in her abilities. It was unclear if most of her teachers cared to know about her academic abilities as long as her behavior was not a disruption. Orlando shared Amber's disdain for attending class when it was unnecessary. Although he attended a traditional public school, he preferred to read books and teach himself. He felt the curriculum provided in schools was limited and he had basically learned all he could in that setting. Because of his views about the limits of formal education, Orlando planned to skip college and work as an apprentice.

Similar to Amber, Vanessa and Tres also dealt with the repercussions of lowered expectations from teachers. As we recounted earlier, Vanessa's responses to the trauma she was facing at home caught the attention of her teachers. Yet far from providing her with additional mental health services or academic support, Vanessa was medicated and placed in special education. She was classified as intellectually disabled, which in the United States indicates that she has an IQ below 70 and has difficulty with daily living skills. Although I did not test Vanessa's IQ, nor would I have considering my concerns about the validity of IQ tests as measures of actual intelligence, I do have a tremendous amount of experience working as a special education teacher. Even without an updated measure of IQ, Vanessa should not be considered intellectually disabled because she was fully self-sufficient in terms of daily living skills. Nonetheless, she had been labeled and sent to special education, a place where many students who display disruptive behaviors or difficulty learning certain concepts find themselves. Special education is well-intentioned, but often misused. It is meant to be a service where students are provided with additional resources to help them access the general education curriculum. However, it can often be a segregated classroom full of students deemed unworthy of the general education system. This includes students with externalizing behaviors, students who learn differently and students who are culturally or linguistically different than the school majority. Up until recently, it was accepted among academics that minority students were overrepresented in special education and this was largely due to teacher bias (Donovan & Cross, 2002; Laura, 2014). Recently, there has been some debate as new studies show minority students may be underrepresented in special education (Farkas et al., 2020). Paul Morgan, a researcher who studied this topic, was quoted as saying, "It's very important to make sure that children are not inappropriately identified as having disabilities based on their race. But equally so, we shouldn't be keeping children from appropriately being identified based on race" (Samuels, 2017). As a former special educator, I find the debate interesting. While I can agree that all students should receive the amount of support necessary for them to be successful in school, it's troubling to me that the argument here is that Black children may actually be more prone to disabilities because of structural inequalities such as growing up in poverty and exposure to lead paint. It may take the spotlight off whether teachers are making special education referrals based on racist bias, but it highlights how systemic racism is detrimental to the health and well-being of Black children from the time they are born, or in actuality from the time they are conceived. As I mentioned earlier, teacher bias does not just present itself in special education referrals. It is also present in discipline responses, suspension rates, levels of support, and interpersonal relationships. While the debate about the role of race in special education referrals will likely continue, Vanessa's classification as intellectually disabled seems unlikely given the level of self-sufficiency and her academic performance in high school.

Tres also admitted to feeling unengaged and unchallenged. At 14, he was already pushing the boundaries of his mother's patience by constantly hanging out with his friends and breaking curfew. Tres spent a lot of time with his friends at a place he referred to as the "clubhouse." Tres described the "clubhouse" as a place where groups of up to 30 teens would come together to discuss things like parties and girls. The idea of 30 teens together immediately concerned me. I, however, was not concerned about them being a danger, but instead how quickly they could become the targets of the police. Tres confirmed my fears when he described what started as a pretty common situation. One day while he was at the clubhouse, one of his friends was cooking and set the smoke detector off. To escape the smoke, Tres and his friends exited the house. When they did, they saw a police car. Tres described the situation in this way:

> And then came from back in the house and opened the windows and I was just standing there and the cop just going to drive past us and looking at us from all corners. He just kept u-turning, u-turning, u-turning. Oh my god whatever. And then the cop come back and started staring at us. He looks out the window and rolls it down and stares. Then he rolls up the window and then he u-turned one more time and didn't u-turn again...because the color of my skin and just because the way I look because some people will tend to see me like an adult or I look like I'm gang affiliated. So like I think it's more likely for me to get stopped than a lot of people because the way I look or the way I act or move. Just like my appearance of and all of that stuff.

Again, Tres refers to his appearance and how it makes him the target of authority figures such as police and prison guards. He knows that because of his complexion, size, and outward appearance, the world doesn't view him as a 14-year-old boy, but instead as someone dangerous. Despite my concerns about the clubhouse, I was happy to hear Tres describe the ongoing conversations about school that occurred there. Tres, like Amber, felt unchallenged at school. He stated:

> One of my main friends that I spend a lot time with now, he be telling me that he feels that classroom got easier to him so, he don't tend to go to school. So, I reach out to him, just go, just to do the work, it's easy credit. It's probably just because it's the first marking period. I mean the second marking period, things might get challenging over time. So, we just being going to school see if it's getting challenging. They haven't. Just, like, when I'm in school, I'll just be doing my work and the teachers, they don't show me attention so I will be on my own doing my work, doing it the way I know how to do it. I'll just be looking at them at them like, what am I supposed to do now? And they'll just be like, "Sit." And I'll just be like, "Okay." And just be sitting there.

The way Tres describes school is the stuff of professional development nightmares. While rigor and engagement are constantly being used as ways teachers can improve their practice, Tres remained unchallenged and unengaged. Delpit (2012) discusses the implications of this type of pedagogy, writing. "...students are quite aware when the instruction they are receiving is subpar. While many are willing to play the game to avoid being challenged, others are distraught at the realization that they are being shortchanged" (p. 75). Both Tres and Amber were willing to allow the subpar instruction or as Delpit writes, they were "willing to play the game." Tres went as far as to say he never aims to score above 75%–80% on an exam because that's considered grade level and that he keeps his homework assignments in his backpack, but rarely turns them in because his teachers don't ask for them. They are there in case a teacher tries to call him out for not doing his work, but if no one asks, Tres doesn't share. If they don't seem to care, Tres responds in kind. Yet, he is aware of the role school will play in his future. While his main goal is to become a D-League basketball player who eventually moves to NBA, he has considered other career options if that does not work out. He expressed an interest in possibly becoming a lawyer, veterinarian, or firefighter and understood that all of those jobs would require some type of diploma or degree.

There have been numerous studies that point to a correlation between parental incarceration and poor educational outcomes. For example, Turney and Haskins (2019) state:

> One study finds that children exposed to parental incarceration, compared to unexposed peers, are more likely to experience grade retention in school. This association is not explained by lower test scores or more behavior problems experienced by children of incarcerated fathers; instead, findings suggest this relationship is driven by teacher's perceptions of children's academic proficiency (Turney & Haskins, 2014). Other studies find that children of incarcerated parents are more likely to be placed in special education (Haskins, 2014) and suspended or expelled from elementary school (Jacobsen, 2016).

> (p. 59)

As illustrated above, poor educational outcomes could be the result of a lack of engagement or from a failure to provide challenging work. It can also be the result of teacher bias. As Gaynes and Krupat (2018) write, "many of these negative effects can be linked to the stigma associated with parental incarceration; in other words, the negative external responses to a parent's incarceration is also damaging to children and families" (p. 182). These findings indicate that schools and educators need to be reflective about their own responsibility in any poor educational outcomes children of incarcerated parents experience. This is not to say that parental incarceration has no effect on children. Parental incarceration has been shown to cause high levels of stress in children, which can lead to depression, anxiety, and other adverse health effects (Gaynes & Krupat, 2018). It is possible the high levels of stress could cause a child to behave poorly in class, including being inattentive, unresponsive, disengaged, or disruptive. Even within my study, some of the collaborators discussed periods of time where their behavior was less than stellar. However, just because parental incarceration is linked with a higher chance of adverse health and educational outcomes, does not mean it must. With the proper support and protective factors in place, the risk of adverse outcomes can be lessened and schools are one of the best places to implement protective factors.

Conclusion

Research shows the children of incarcerated parents may experience many issues at school including externalizing and internalizing behavior and poor academic performance and outcomes. While much of the research has associated these behaviors with parental incarceration, it is worth examining how school-based support or lack thereof mitigates or exacerbates these behaviors. As Shlafer et al. state, "It is possible that the cumulative effect of stigmatization and negative interactions at school, combined with family risks, contributes to a disinclination to persist in academic endeavors" (p. 108). Schools need to do a better job of making sure they are safe spaces for all students, particularly children of incarcerated parents who benefit greatly from a supportive environment.

References

American Civil Liberties Union. (2018). *11 million days lost: Race, discipline, and safety at U.S. public schools.*

Burton, L. (2007). Childhood adultification in economically disadvantaged families: A conceptual model. *Family relations, 56*(4), 329–345.

Ciccone, A., Dallaire, D., & Wilson, L. (2010). Teacher's experiences with and expectations of children with incarcerated Parents. *Journal of Applied Developmental Psychology, 31*, 281–290.

Darling-Hammond, L. (1998). *Unequal opportunity: Race and education.* Brookings. Washington, D.C.

Donovan, M.S., & Cross, C.T. (Eds.) (2002). *Minority students in special and gifted education.* Washington, D.C.: National Academy Press, National Research Council Committee on Minority Representation in Special Education.

Delpit, L. (2012). *"Multiplication is for white people": Raising expectations for other people's children.* New York, NY: The New Press.

Farkas, G., Morgan, P.L., Hillemeier, M.M., Mitchell, C., & Woods, A.D. (2020). District-level achievement gaps explain Black and Hispanic over-representation in special education. *Exceptional Children, 86*(4), 374–392.

Flannery, M.E. (2015). The school to prison pipeline: Time to shut it down. *neaToday,* 42–45.

Gaynes, E., & Krupat, T. (2018). Minimizing the impact of parental incarceration. In E. Drucker (Ed.), *Decarcerating America: From mass punishment to public health* (pp. 179–200). New York, NY: The New Press.

Henning, K. (2017). Boys to men: The role of policing in the socialization of black boys. In A. Davis (Ed.), *Policing the black man* (pp. 57–87). New York, NY: Pantheon Books.

Institute of Education Sciences. (2019). Status and trends in the education of racial and ethnic groups 2018. U.S. Department of Education.

Jacobsen, W.C. (2016). Punished for their fathers? School discipline among children of the prison boom. *Fragile Families Working Paper #WP14-08-FF.*

Laura, C. T. (2014). *Being bad: My baby brother and the school-to-prison pipeline.* New York, NY: Teachers College Press.

Lyiscott, J. (2019). *Black appetite. White food. Issues of race, voice and justice within and beyond the classroom.* New York, NY: Routledge.

Mark, C. (2020). *A belief in meritocracy is not only false; it's bad for you.* Princeton, NJ: Princeton University Press.

Miller, J. (2021). 'This ain't Utah:' Advocates led by Paris Hilton urge law-makers to pass reforms for 'troubled-teen' treatment centers. *The Salt Lake Tribune.*

Morris, M. W. (2019). Countering the adultification of Black girls. *Educational Leadership, 76*(7), 44–48.

National Center for Education Statistics. (2020). Characteristics of public school teachers. U.S. Department of Education.

National Center for Education Statistics. (2020). Fast facts: Bullying. U.S. Department of Education.

National Resource Center on Children and Families of the Incarcerated. (2014). Fact sheet.

Pember, M.A. (2019). Death by civilization. *The Atlantic.*

Samuels, C.A. (2017). Minority students still missing out on special education, new analysis says. *Education Week.*

Scharffer, K. (2021). Racial, ethnic diversity increases yet again with the 117th Congress. Pew Center Research.

Shedd, C. (2015). *Unequal city: Race, schools, and perceptions on injustice.* New York, NY: Russell Sage Foundation.

Shlafer, R.J., Davis, L., & Dallaire, D.H. (2019). Parental incarceration during middle childhood and adolescence. In J.M. Eddy & J. Poehlmann-Tynan (Eds.), *Handbook on children with incarcerated parents: Research, policy and practice* (pp. 101–116). Switzerland: Springer Nature.

Spector, C. (2019). Racial disparities in school are linked to the achievement gap between Black and white students nationwide, according to Stanford-led study. Stanford Graduate School of Education.

Terada, Y. (2021). Why Black teachers walk away. George Lucas Educational Foundation.

The Educational Opportunity Monitoring Project. Racial and ethnic achievement gaps. Stanford Center for Education and Policy Analysis.

The Legal Center for Foster Care and Education. (2018). Fostering success in education: Nationalfactsheet on the educational outcomes of children in foster care. FosterEd.

Turney, K., & Haskins, A.R. (2019). Parental incarceration and children's well-being: Findings from the fragile families and child well-being study. In J.M. Eddy & J. Poehlmann- Tynan (Eds.), *Handbook on children with incarcerated parents: Research, policy and practice* (pp. 53–64). Switzerland: Springer Nature.

U.S. Department of Education. (2020). Students in foster care. Administrators.

4 Supporting Children of Incarcerated Parents

Creating Safe Spaces in Schools and Becoming an Ally

> I only told one teacher because I see her like a mother to me and I'm really close to her. I just felt comfortable speaking to her about it 'cuz I remember she was like what are you doing over the weekend? I was like I'm going to go see my dad all the way upstate. She's like your dad doesn't live with you? And I felt like she would have thought my mom or dad are divorced or something so I was like "No, he's incarcerated." She said she had someone in her family in jail too so I just felt comfortable talking to her about it.
>
> (Jacqueline)

The Role of Schooling

Throughout the course of their education, children in the United States will spend about 13 years in school. Because of the large number of children that schools serve and the amount of time children spend there, schools have the unique ability to have a substantial influence on our country and its citizens. And while almost everyone can agree that access to education is positive, there is less agreement over whether schools have been fulfilling their role in our society. In 2018, "Senate Committee on Health, Education, Labor and Pensions Chair Lamar Alexander (R-TN) said the role of American public education is 'to teach reading, writing, arithmetic and what it means to be an American citizen'" (Arnett, p. 1). Democratic representative Danny Davis, similarly stated that schools should be doing more to teach about American democracy and how to move it forward. While these assertions may sound reasonable, they are in some ways quite exclusionary. What does it mean to be an American citizen? How do we move forward democracy? Unfortunately, even students of color whose families have been here for generations are not always viewed as full-fledged Americans. This is evident in the calls for Black Americans

DOI: 10.4324/9781003202141-5

to "go home" when they speak up about racism in this country, as if this country is not their home. President Obama and more recently Vice President Harris both had their citizenship status questioned despite being born in the United States. John McCain who ran against Obama was born in the Panama Canal Zone, then under US control. Mr. McCain was an American citizen like President Obama. However, Mr. McCain was born outside the physical borders of the United States and there was little discussion about his citizenship status. President Obama was born in Hawaii, but the news coverage about his birthplace was so pervasive he eventually released his birth certificate to quell the rumors. The difference between Mr. McCain and President Obama was race. Even with a native-born white parent, President Obama was not viewed as American by some of the people in this country simply because he was Black. If one believes that American citizen is synonymous with white Anglo Saxon Protestant, then many schools have in fact been teaching children what it means to be an American citizen, but unfortunately many students will never be able to reach that goal simply because their skin isn't white. Rep. Davis' comments about moving American democracy forward are also interesting. Moving democracy forward would require an earnest attempt to live up to the ideals of our nation; *with liberty and justice for all.* In order to do that, we must acknowledge our problems both historically and presently. Racism, sexism, xenophobia, and other forms of discrimination should be taught as facts. Instead, some schools won't even discuss the topics while others actively engage in perpetuating the discrimination. In 2019, the *1619 Project* was released by the New York Times. The project, developed by journalist Nikole Hannah-Jones, reimagined 1619, the year the first enslaved person arrived in colonial Virginia, as the beginning of American history. While some educators and schools welcomed the curriculum as a much needed resource to supplement traditional curricula which tend to briefly touch upon slavery and view its consequences as in the past, others condemned the project as anti-American. It sparked such controversy that then president Donald J. Trump commissioned a committee to write and release the *1776 Report*, intended to support "patriotic education" (Clifton, 2021). The meaning of patriotic is this context is much the same as Senator Alexander's comments about American citizens; patriotic education glorifies the role of white people in this country while ignoring other groups' contributions and the damage the racism has caused. Rick Santorum, a former presidential candidate and current CNN contributor echoed this sentiment recently when speaking at an event for conservative youth. Santorum stated, "We came here and created a blank slate. We birthed a nation from nothing. I mean, there was nothing here. I mean, yes, we have Native Americans but candidly there isn't much Native American culture in American culture" (Lock, 2021, p. 1). What Santorum failed to mention was that the "blank slate" was created through genocide and the lack, or perceived lack, of Native American culture in American culture is due to the strategic whitewashing of our history. This type of thinking displays why goals such as teaching students what it means to be an American citizen in schools can actually be harmful. If people do not consider Native Americans as Americans, who can really be considered American?

Schools should and could be sites where the solutions to society's ills are conceived and practiced, if only we are brave enough to make them that way. Angela Davis (2003) wrote, "Schools can therefore be seen as the most powerful alternative to jails and prison" (p. 108). However, she was quick to add,

> Unless the current structures of violence are eliminated from schools in impoverished communities of color – including the presence of armed security guards and police – and unless schools become places that encourage the joy of learning, these schools will remain major conduits to prison.
>
> (p. 108)

In some ways, schools do illustrate what it means to be an American citizen. To be an American citizen is to exist in an inequitable system where race, socio-economic status, and other factors often determine how people will treat you and what you have access to. Students are receiving this type of education even if they aren't aware of it. To progress toward democracy, schools must look past the status quo and the distorted version of Americanism we have come to accept, and begin to create spaces where all students feel valued and equity is considered a foundation of school culture. Spaces, that as Davis stated, encourage the "joy" of learning. This may sound like a lofty goal and it is, especially considering the history of schooling and the explicit racism present in American society. However, if we truly want to improve not only student outcomes, but society, it is a goal we must work toward. And while this book and this chapter in particular, are dedicated to improving educational outcomes for children of incarcerated parents, strategies for children of incarcerated parents often mirror best practices for all students. Creating a community of respect, where students feel valued, engaged, and challenged is not unique to children of incarcerated parents. Best practices are best practices for all. It is important to understand this because educators don't need to know, nor should they wait until they are certain they have children of incarcerated parents in their classroom to begin implementing these practices. In fact, many teachers will teach children of incarcerated parents without ever knowing their parental situation. This is understandable considering studies have shown that teacher expectations decrease once they become aware a student has an incarcerated parent (Ciccone et al., 2010). Therefore, even if one is not certain that they have children of incarcerated parents in their classroom, these suggestions can still be implemented because while children of incarcerated parents are a unique population, the core of this chapter is recognizing the humanity and dignity of all children. In the previous chapter, it was evident that for the youth in my study, school was generally not a positive experience. It was treated was a required event that the youth needed to engage with to accomplish their long-term goals. However, the youth did have some positive spaces in their school experience that I will highlight as we discuss how to support children of incarcerated parents in schools and push our democracy forward through anti-racist and humanizing pedagogy.

Foster Positive Relationships

There is a perception of educators, a majority female profession, as nurturing and kind so this suggestion may seem obvious to some. However, educators are people and people are not always kind. Everyone is entitled to a bad day here and there and I had my fair share when I was in the classroom. However, overall I was kind to my students. The kindness I showed them created a safe space and set the foundation for our relationship. When I use the word kind, I am referring to the ability to be humane. When I speak of kindness, I am speaking of being loving toward children and displaying care and concern for their well-being. Respect and empathy are a part of kindness. They should be a part of teaching as well. As Delpit (2012) states:

> When students believe that the teacher cares for them and is concerned about them, they will frequently rise to the expectations set. When students believe that teachers believe in their ability, when they see teachers willing to go the extra mile to meet their academic deficiencies, they are much more likely to try.
>
> (p. 82)

Given the fact that research shows teachers have lowered expectations for children of incarcerated parents, Delpit's assertion is extremely powerful. Students tend to live up to teacher expectations; if a teacher believes a student can do something, the student will try to meet their expectations. Sometimes the greatest tool an educator has to help improve student outcomes is to change their own behavior. Educators should question the level of expectations they have for students and why. If their expectations are lower for some students than others, the educator should be reflective about the reason for this. Lowered expectations are not harmless. Students know when teachers have them. For example, Tres stated:

> I told the school that the work is easy and I showed them the work, I just never turned it in. So like some of the work I was passing my classes, but the classes I'm not passing, I have the work in my bag and I never turned it in. But they [the teachers] know I'm fully capable of doing the work.

While Tres believes his teachers are aware he is capable of completing his work, they seem to have the expectation that he won't do it. Tres, in turn, is living up to their expectations by failing to hand in the assignments he completed despite them being present in his backpack. Despite his teacher's assumptions, Tres keeps completing his work and has it ready at a moment's notice should someone care enough to ask for it. Throughout Tres' interview he maintained a jovial disposition and a somewhat nonchalant attitude toward school. However, it was obvious through his statements that he knew the importance of school, often discussing it with his friends and mentioning numerous times that he wished to be challenged more. Tres believed in himself, but he felt his teachers did not. While many of my youth collaborators found one adult at school who seemed to genuinely care about them and their future, Tres did not. Perhaps this is the reason he seemed to have lowest grades out of the youth I interviewed and seemed the most unclear about his future plans.

Although Tres' school experience and lack of adult support was disconcerting, most the youth collaborators were able to find support in their school building. Even Amber, the student who spent most of her time roaming the halls because she felt unchallenged in school had a favorite teacher. She stated:

> There's like this one teacher at every school. If you disrespect her, the kids are just going to punch you in your throat. That's that teacher. I swear. One of the kids disrespected her one day and my best friend threw a chair at him. I just sat there and said yep, now get out. She's so nice and different. There's no reason why you should disrespect her. If you are, these kids in that school will probably murder you. There's a known fact that they will.

Amber, who enjoyed getting trying to elicit a reaction from people, including me, peppered her statement with violence, which is what some may highlight from that exchange. However, beyond that is a message. The teacher she was describing was "different" than most teachers and because of that, the students protected her. The teacher was different because she was "nice." Imagine what experiences these children must have had in school that having a nice teacher is seen as an anomaly. Amber and the other students in her class were fiercely protective of the one adult in the building who showed them kindness. Amber also identified this teacher as a role model, sharing that she had numerous degrees and loved to do outdoor activities. It was clear that while Amber did not enjoy attending school overall, she felt a special bond with this teacher who showed a genuine interest in her students and treated them in a way that others did not.

Despite identifying adults in the building that they could trust, none of the youth I interviewed described a situation where incarceration was brought up as a topic in class or other school settings. They chose to share with certain adults in the building because they felt those adults truly cared about them. While I advocate for normalizing discussions about incarceration as part of the classroom experience, it is also worth noting that the youth were motivated to share because they recognized a kind adult who they felt they could trust. For anyone struggling with how to best support children of incarcerated parents in the classroom, perhaps the biggest step we can take is creating an environment where they want, seek, and accept our support. This includes creating a culture of respect and humanity; an environment where positive relationships are the foundation.

Be Authentic

In teacher preparation programs, there are often discussions about how to present yourself in front of the classroom. There was a period when people thought it was sound advice to tell future teachers not to smile for six months in attempt to gain control over the classroom and make the students take them seriously. It is most likely still advice being given out today and somewhere a new teacher is thinking that if they happen to crack a smile prior to Christmas, their class will descend into chaos. I have worked in a teacher preparation program for quite some time and I find this advice to be counterproductive. When I was in the classroom, I smiled daily. It came naturally and the times when I smiled the hardest were the times I remember the most. The classroom was not out of control or in chaos. It was an engaging space where students were happy to be and they could tell I was happy to be with them. Teaching should not require a person to create a whole new character. Not only would that would be exhausting to do daily, but it is also pointless. Attempting to trick the students into believing that you are someone that you are not is a breach of that relationship. Educators ask students to show up and be their authentic selves and they must be brave enough to do the same. If educators truly believe that youth are competent actors and meaning makers in their own lives, they must trust that they can interact and coexist with a variety of people and personalities; not just a cookie-cutter version of what a teacher should be.

In the introduction, I spoke to how an honest conversation with my students allowed them to share details about their personal life that I wasn't privy to prior. This information was invaluable to me as a teacher because it not only strengthened our relationship, but it allowed me to support them in ways I hadn't considered before. It was a mutual exchange of trust and vulnerability and it allowed me to become a better educator. It was an authentic moment that I wouldn't have had if I had subscribed to the belief that authenticity and vulnerability are incompatible with teaching. Instead, I would argue that authenticity and vulnerability are part of what makes great teachers. It is also a great tool to help support children of incarcerated parents who may be hiding their true feelings in order to avoid uncomfortable conversations or to make other people feel better. This is a heavy burden for them to carry and when we model trust and vulnerability, we show children of incarcerated parents ways to help heal their own trauma.

Authenticity can also present itself in the ability to have honest conversations with students. If students feel that you are an educator that genuinely cares about their well-being and have been honest with them in the past, they are more likely to listen to your advice and be open to difficult conversations. For example, Emmanuel had dreams of becoming an athlete, but his grades needed to improve. He credits an honest discussion with one of his teachers for helping him get back on track. He stated:

> One day I was in 7th grade and I had a conversation with my math teacher and he showed me the averages I would need to go D-1 and I saw my averages so I was like I have to step my game up. In 8th grade my grades got higher. He saw my basketball game and thought I was pretty good so for him to see my average he was like wow. He said you could be really nice but I had to

change my grades. When I saw my average it was at an 84 and I was like 5 points away from going D-1 but I know it's not too late. I know this second semester I have to get up to at least a 90 average

Emmanuel's teacher took a genuine interest in him and supported his goals. However, his support included having an authentic conversation with Emmanuel about where he was and where he needed to be to achieve his goals. The teacher continued to support Emmanuel by attending his games. I am happy to report that Emmanuel will begin college in the fall of 2021 and has been recruited to play football at a Division 1 school. Although Emmanuel deserves much of the credit, he never forgot the teacher who cared enough to have an honest conversation with him.

It is important for educators to interact with students as their authentic self. Children can often tell when someone is being disingenuous or phony. In order to build strong relationship with children and earn their trust, educators must model honesty. If they begin the relationship pretending to be someone else, then the foundation of that relationship is deception. A relationship in which educators want the level of trust it would require for a child to share their most personal information, such as the incarceration of a parent or loved one, cannot begin with a falsehood.

Be Reflective

All people have biases. Some of our biases may be clear to us while others live beneath the surface. While biases are potentially harmful, implicit or unconscious biases are particularly concerning because it is difficult to address stereotypical assumptions if you are not aware that you have them. Writing for the White House in 2008, Handelsman and Sakaney state:

> A lifetime of experience and cultural history shapes people and their judgments of others. Research demonstrates that most people hold unconscious, implicit assumptions that influence their judgments and perceptions of others. Implicit bias manifests in expectations or assumptions about physical or social characteristics dictated by stereotypes that are based on a person's race, gender, age, or ethnicity. People who intend to be fair, and believe they are egalitarian, apply biases unintentionally. Some behaviors that result from implicit bias manifest in actions, and others are

embodied in the absence of action; either can reduce the quality of the workforce and create an unfair and destructive environment.

(p. 1)

Like any other person, educators hold biases and when they are unaware of their biases this can lead to environments that are not safe for all students. Biases can lead to actions that negatively impact a child's school experience. It is difficult for students to feel fully comfortable in a classroom where the teacher is treating them differently based on conscious or unconscious preconceptions. These preconceptions often affect already marginalized groups such as students of color, students with disabilities, students from low-socio-economic backgrounds, students who are undocumented and students who are a part of the LGBTQ+ community. Biases also have a large impact on children of incarcerated parents and other people directly impacted by mass incarceration. As previously discussed, there are many negative assumptions made about those involved in the criminal justice system and these assumptions are also sometimes used to view their family and loved ones as well. Therefore, it is important for educators to address any explicit or implicit biases they may hold about incarcerated people, formerly incarcerated people and their families because these biases can impact how they interact with children of incarcerated parents. Turney (2019) writes, "these children often experience a (conscious or unconscious) social stigma from their teachers and classmates that stems directly from their parents' incarceration. Educational institutions can help in reducing this stigma" (p. 25). If an educator feels that they are unable to properly support a child because of their own biases or lack of knowledge on a topic, it's advisable for them to search for someone within the building who can better support the child. While educators should always be mindful of privacy concerns, school guidance counselors and social workers may have more experience with the topic and be able to offer additional support.

Having biases doesn't make someone a bad person. However, an unwillingness to address potential biases that are harmful to others while working in a position where your attitudes and actions affect the emotional health of children daily is unacceptable. Children of incarcerated parents, who are disproportionately Black or brown and poor are already subject to biases daily and have been since birth. Parental incarceration adds an additional layer of judgment and stigma. Reflective educators who are willing to do the difficult work of addressing their own shortcomings have the least chance of causing harm and the best chance of supporting children of incarcerated parents in schools.

Be Conscious

In order to support children of incarcerated parents and other students affected by traumatic events, an educator must be aware of potential issues that may arise in schools. When educators create assignments, they should avoid assumptions about family dynamics. Creating a card for Mother's Day or Father's Day may seem like an enjoyable task, but for students who are unable to spend holidays with their parents, it may bring up difficult feelings. This is not to say that these types of tasks cannot be done in schools, but that they should be implemented with more care. Having a conversation about what these holidays are actually intended to do can broaden the types of people children may consider making cards for and alleviate some stress. For example, if an educator explains that these holidays are intended to celebrate people in our lives who provide us with nurturing and support, students may choose to make a card for their grandparent, extended family member, community member or even their teacher. If they choose to make a card for their parent, but experience a shift in emotion while doing it, teachers can provide them with the space to express themselves. This could include a private conversation or allowing the student to spend some time alone for a few minutes. The most important part is that the educator recognizes that not all families are the same and plans to give the students the space to complete the assignment in a way that feels comfortable to them.

In the situation have we just discussed, it may be beneficial for the teacher to bring in a book or other tools to aid the conversation. The benefits of using books to help people learn about difficult topics are well documented. Bibliotherapy is a type of reading that can be used as a tool for healing and help students get navigate difficult times. Khalik (2017) states, "The goal of bibliotherapy is to broaden and deepen the children' understanding of a particular problem that requires attention" (p. 31). Ford et al. (2019) note that for Black people, reading has been used as a source of freedom and healing since the days of slavery. They state:

> Throughout history, literacy among Black people has been an act of resistance that is liberating and mentally healing. During slavery, anti-literacy laws prohibited the education of slaves as a means to control them and prevent rebellion. If a slave attempted to learn how to read, they risked being punished, sold, or potentially death (Williams, 2009). However, despite it being illegal, Black people knew that learning to read was a tool that could

grant them a mental escape, even if temporary. But for some, reading led to physical freedom. Lerner (1973) described a story of a slave woman in Natchez, Louisiana, who taught others to read and write, which allowed many of them to later write their own passes and escape to Canada. However, for many slaves, access to written words, regardless of genre, provided mental freedom and the ability to see themselves in a world where they had no power over their circumstances (see Williams). Therapeutic reading has been and continues to be a technique individuals and therapists use to understand, escape from, push through, or acquire a solution for adverse circumstances.

(p. 55)

The use of bibliotherapy continues today and is often employed by educators. For example, a teacher may read *Stick and Stone* by Beth Ferry to support children impacted by bullying or *Anti-Racist Baby* by Ibram X. Kendi to start a dialogue about racism and discrimination. There are a variety of children's books available that discuss varying family structures, including an increasing number of books about families where a parent is incarcerated. Jacqueline Woodson's picture book *Visiting Day* is one of the most well-known books to feature a family dealing with parental incarceration. It has beautiful illustrations that engage young eyes and approaches the topic of incarceration with care and love. There are a growing number of books for all ages that can be used in classrooms to foster conscious conversations about incarceration and other difficult topics. I authored a book titled *Anna's Test* which is meant to highlight the positive ways in which families stay connected during incarceration and illustrate that while parental incarceration is a big part of a child's life, it is not the only part of their life. Books such as *Stardust: We Always Share the Same Sky* by Ivana Mlinac and *Far Apart, Close in Heart* by Becky Birtha are also excellent read alouds that deal with incarceration. The Osborne Association provides a list of books featuring children of incarcerated parents on their website and has separated the list based on intended audience age. While the books I have mentioned are picture books, there are also young adult novels that deal with parental incarceration as well such as *Ruby on the Outside* by Nora Raleigh Baskin. When using books as a way to foster conversation in the classroom, it is important that teachers do not single students out even if they are aware that student may be impacted by incarceration. Mass incarceration and its collateral consequences affect everyone. Reading a book about parental incarceration may help a child with an incarcerated parent feel represented, but it may also cause other children who aren't directly impacted to learn about the topic or confront any biases they may have surrounding it. Engaging in these conversations just isn't beneficial for the child with an incarcerated parent; it is beneficial to any classroom whose goal is a culture of care and respect.

That being said, it is important to review the books being presented before reading them. It is easy to google books that feature a child with an incarcerated parent and buy the first one that presents itself. There is an assumption at times that because a book addresses a topic, that it addresses it well. Parental incarceration is a sensitive topic and one that should be handled with care. Educators should review the books and any resources they plan to share with students to analyze them or any implicit assumptions or possible triggers. For example, when I was completing my dissertation, I was interested in exploring the literature available to children. At the time, I was still working in the classroom and I was eager to receive the books so I could use them for my study and my students. I typed the necessary keywords into the Amazon search bar and went on quite the ordering spree. When I received one of the books, I was immediately disturbed. The cover, the one piece of a book that is meant to immediately grab the attention of the reader, featured a brick wall background. A two-dimensional male face appeared over the bricks and lines meant to represent bars cut across the face. I had to consider the purpose of this illustration. The book was about supporting children of incarcerated parents, yet the cover was triggering. And while there was helpful information inside of the book, I couldn't help but think how off-putting the cover may be for youth who are concerned about their parent's well-being while incarcerated. When I wrote *Anna's Test*, I wrote it with intentionality and published it in the same way. Both myself and the illustrator, Kianga Peterson professionally known as Kiki Kitty, are directly impacted individuals. It was meant to be a beautifully illustrated book because children enjoy reading stories with great illustrations. It was also designed to be a book that can be read as an enjoyable story instead of only being used to discuss incarceration. Yes, I wanted children of incarcerated parents to feel represented and yes I wanted to normalize conversations about incarceration, but in my eyes the best way to do that was by creating a book that children *want* to read; a book that catches someone's eye and then keeps them engaged with a relatable story. Educators may not be able to get that type of background about every book they choose, but a quick read should give them an idea of whether it is a book that supports children of incarcerated parents as opposed to just being about children of incarcerated parents.

Be an Ally

With the civil unrest that occurred in the spring of 2020 after the murders of George Floyd and Breonna Taylor, there was a focus on how to be an ally to Black people. Being an ally includes using one's position or privilege to support the cause of another person or group. While we all have varying levels of privilege, within a school building, the faculty tend to have more power than the students. This is because the structure of schools is usually quite authoritarian, even if police aren't present. The adults in the building, particularly the teachers and principals are the authority figures. Traditionally, students are expected to submit to the authority of the adults in the building with little resistance.

Vivett Dukes, a veteran educator in New York City and founder of Speak Ya Truth, is an ally and advocate for children of incarcerated parents. While she never experienced parental incarceration herself, Vivett is married to John Dukes, a father who spent over 20 years incarcerated in a New York Prison. Watching John parent from behind bars allowed Vivett to witness how deep the connection between parent and child can remain during incarceration. While Vivett has always been a progressive educator, she credits her marriage with helping her see the challenges that children of incarcerated parents face and facilitating her role as ally in her school building. John has been released from prison and is now home, but when he was incarcerated, Vivett visited him regularly. While she loved seeing her husband, the visits were exhausting due to factors like the distance she was required to travel and the process for entrance. One day when Vivett was waiting to visit John, she noticed a student from her school in the line. Vivett had to make a choice. She could pretend she did not see the student or she could interact with them. Vivett chose to speak with the student and share that she was visiting her husband. The student shared that she was visiting a family member as well. After the visit, Vivett began to think of the stress visiting put on her and how exhausted she was when she had to return to work on Monday. This made her rethink her interactions with students. Sometimes children would return from the weekend exhausted. Many would put their heads down on the desk. Vivett realized that she didn't know what her students had to go through physically and emotionally over the weekend before returning to school on Monday. She decided to extend grace and encourages other educators to do the same.

In addition to being understanding, educators can actively signal their support in a variety of ways. One way is by displaying the

Children of Incarcerated Parent's Bill of Rights in a prominent location in their classroom. The Bill of Rights was created in 2005 in San Francisco by young people with the assistance of their adult allies and has since been used all over the country to advocate for the rights of children of incarcerated parents. By displaying it in their classrooms, educators and other school staff can send a non-verbal message to all students that (1) they are aware of the topic and (2) they are supportive allies. Vivett likens the display of the Rights as akin to the light in windows for enslaved people attempting to travel along the underground railroad. Vivett stated, "They know that this is a safe space without ever having to say a word." I found this to be true. I was once working in a school different than my own during the summer and happened to be in the parent coordinator's office. When I looked around, I noticed the Children of Incarcerated Parent's Bill of Rights hanging on the wall. I was pleased that Vivett was correct. I automatically felt as if there was an ally in the building who was at least somewhat aware of the topic.

Another way that adults can act as allies in schools is by using humanizing language. There has been a lot of pushback against the use of the terms felon, inmate, and convict. The work being done in this area is having an effect as some media outlets and even some businesses have started to use people first language such as person who is/was incarcerated. Recently, Dr. Abigail Henson, a criminology professor at Arizona State University, noted her surprise when she received a call from an incarcerated person and the recording did not refer to them as an inmate. She wrote,

> Had call from SCI Phoenix. Usually the Securus robot says "call from X, an inmate at..." But, this time, instead of "inmate" the robot said "incarcerated individual." Privatization of prison calls is a whole other issue, but I was pleasantly surprised by this humanizing change.
>
> (Henson, 2021)

Language is a small adjustment that can have a huge impact. By actively choosing not to use words that dehumanize, educators can act as allies to children of incarcerated parents. When discussing their incarcerated parent with a child, it is quite easy to just use the term parent, mom or dad. It is also important to use these terms, not just when speaking to the child, but also when speaking with other adults in the building. Other adults will begin to use the language you model and if they don't, there are ways to have respectful conversations about the appropriate terminology. The focus should be on what's best for the youth and not what the adults are used to doing.

Be Willing to Learn

As educators, we should be lifelong learners. Things are constantly developing and changing, and this requires educators to have a willingness to learn new information. At times, having a conversation with a child or children about incarceration may seem frightening or uncomfortable, depending on one's proximity to the topic. A topic should not be avoided just because it makes the teacher uncomfortable. There are numerous resources that will educate people who are willing to learn. For example, the *Handbook on Children with Incarcerated Parents: Research Policy, and Practice* (2019) edited by J. Mark Eddy and Julie Poehlmann-Tynan features 25 chapters all dedicated to research on children of incarcerated parents. The book is comprehensive and is a good resource looking for someone who is interested in all aspects of parental incarceration. There are also books like Sylvia A. Harvey's *The Shadow System: Mass Incarceration and the American Family* (2020) which takes a journalistic approach to documenting the experiences of families impacted by the criminal justice system. Anye Young's book *Teen Guide to Living with Incarcerated Parents* (2018) offers the perspective of a teen impacted by parental incarceration. Organizations such as We Got Us Now, Speak Ya Truth, POPS the Club, Osborne Association, International Coalition for Children with Incarcerated Parents, New Hour Amachi, Dream Academy, and the National Resource Center on Children and Families of the Incarcerated have websites that provide countless free resources. Documentaries such as Tres, Maison, and Dasan by filmmaker Denali Tiller provide a visual of the experiences of children of incarcerated parents. The information is available for those who are interested in learning.

As a directly impacted individual who researched children of incarcerated parents and received a doctorate for that research, I still don't know everything there is to know about children of incarcerated parents. The day I claim that I do is probably the day I should stop doing the work. Things are constantly changing and progressing. Not knowing everything shouldn't stop someone from supporting children of incarcerated parents or engaging in this work. An unwillingness to learn should. If an educator truly feels that they are not well versed enough in the topic, then support can look a variety of ways. Perhaps the educator could research organizations and resources with the child. At minimum, the educator can be present. The power of presence should never be underestimated and sometimes a listening ear is the best medicine.

Programs and Curricula

Most support for children of incarcerated parents is provided by outside organizations. The students may attend these organizations outside of school or the organization may bring activities into the school. For example, POPS (Pain of the Prison System) the club is a non-profit that operates in several schools around the United States. The mission of POPS the club is "to create a safe, empowering space in high schools for the children and other loved ones of the incarcerated" (POPS the Club, 2021, p. 1). The clubs produce anthologies written by directly impacted youth that could be an excellent tool for bibliotherapy. Other organizations support children of incarcerated parents during after-school hours. For example, the Osborne Association is home to the Youth Action Council (YAC), a youth-led advocacy group that seeks change often based on their personal experience with parental incarceration. Based in New York, the group has seen success with the passage of legislation such as Ashley's Law, which requires the New York State Department of Corrections and Community Supervision (DOCCS) to give the public information regarding the specific visiting rules at more than 50 state prisons in New York. In 2021, April's Bill, another piece of legislation also known as the Proximity Bill was signed into law by NY Governor Andrew Cuomo. This law requires DOCCS to consider the home location of an incarcerated parent's children before deciding where to place the parent. Legislation like this is being introduced throughout the United States and is often led by youth with the support of their allies. Becoming familiar with the local organizations in their area that support children of incarcerated parents can provide educators with a valuable asset to foster the support of children of incarcerated parents in schools.

Educators may also be looking to provide more in school support for children of incarcerated parents. Unfortunately, there are not many widely known curricula available for teachers specifically dedicated to children of incarcerated parents. Trauma-informed curricula may make mention of parental incarceration, but cover other topics as well. After-school and out-of-school programs may utilize their own curriculums that may or may not be appropriate for an in-school setting. I noticed this gap during my time doing this work and co-authored a curriculum with Pamela Brunskill titled *Joining Forces: A School-Based Support Circle for Directly Impacted Children*. Pamela and I are both directly impacted educators and set out to assist other educators who may want to support children of incarcerated parents in schools, but aren't sure how. If there is a comparable curriculum, I have not seen it as of yet. That however does not mean it doesn't exist. It could just mean that it wasn't easily discoverable to me during my search. Either way, there is a definite need for more curricula to support teachers who want to support children of incarcerated parents in schools. I hope to see many more available in the future.

Differences in Children of Incarcerated Parents

The response to a parent's incarceration will vary from child to child even if they are siblings or live in the same household. Age can be a huge factor in how a child responds to their parent's incarceration and it should be a consideration when educators are thinking of how to best support children of incarcerated parents. While honesty and transparency are key, it is possible that an educator may be aware of a parent's incarceration when the child is not. This is particularly true of younger children who are more likely to believe that their parent is away on a vacation or college or perhaps left for a long work assignment. If this is the case, it is not the educator's decision to share that information with the child. It is the decision of the parents and caregivers. There are multiple reasons why a parent or caregiver may choose to hide the truth from a child and while I advocate for being honest in a developmentally appropriate way for all children, I am respectful of the guardian's decision. Children who are separated from their parents at a young age, for example, birth to three years old, may develop attachment issues (Besemer et al., 2019). Primary school-aged children, particularly boys, are said to display more externalizing disruptive behaviors, i.e. fighting, breaking things, than their peers who have not experienced parental incarceration. Older children may seem withdrawn and suffer from depressive symptoms (Turney & Goodsell, 2018). Another factor in a child's response to incarceration is whether the incarcerated parent lived with them prior to incarceration. If the parent did, their absence may cause financial disruptions and affect their living situation. When a father is incarcerated, the child is more likely to remain living with their mother. When a mother is incarcerated the child is more likely to live with an extended relative or enter foster care (Burnson & Weymouth, 2019). In addition, the length of a sentence and the child's proximity to their parent can affect their response as well. A child who is separated from their parent for a year or less may react differently than a child whose parent receives a sentence of 20 or more years. If the child is able to speak to or see their parent regularly their response to incarceration may be different than a child who has not seen or spoke to a parent in an extended period of time. The experiences of children of incarcerated parents are so varied and depend on so many factors that their response is almost impossible to predict or generalize. However, the strategies mentioned above are best practices in general and can assist all children of incarcerated parents in schools. It is also important to note that just because a child doesn't have an incarcerated parent, that doesn't not mean they have not been impacted by mass incarceration. Children who have experienced the incarceration of siblings, aunts or uncles, grandparents, and other loved ones are affected too. Children who formerly had an incarcerated parent, but the parent has since been released can still benefit from support. The collateral consequences of mass incarceration cannot be limited to biological parents who are currently incarcerated. Mass incarceration has far reaching consequences that touches society as a whole, not just those behind bars.

Conclusion

There is a lot of work that needs to be done in order to have the school system live up to its full potential. While there are many schools and educators, both historically and presently, who have engaged in the revolutionary work of creating a more equitable society and educating youth about what a true democracy would look like, the system itself has a foundation of white supremacy. This should not discourage anyone from the task of eradicating oppression and discrimination in schools. As educators, we have to be conscious of the ways schools and the people who inhabit them, ourselves included, perpetuate harmful systems, policies, and perceptions. As Turney (2019) writes,

> Given the link between parental incarceration and children's well-being, as well as the fact that children spend a substantial amount of time in school, schools provide a unique opportunity to intervene and aid children who have currently or formerly incarcerated parents.
>
> (p. 25)

It is time schools began using this opportunity. Although large-scale change is needed, there are things that can be done on an individual level to support children of incarcerated parents and other marginalized children. If we want to teach, we must be willing to teach all children. We must love all children. We must be willing to put progress over discomfort and show up daily to fight systems that dim the light of some so that others may appear brighter. This is the work. This is the role of schools.

References

Besemer, K.L., Dennison, S.M., Bijleveld, C., & Murray, J. (2019). Effects of parental incarceration on children: Lessons from international research. In J.M. Eddy & J. Poehlmann-Tynan (Eds.), *Handbook on children with incarcerated parents: Research, policy and practice* (pp. 65–81). Switzerland: Springer Nature.

Burnson, C., & Weymouth, L. (2019). Infants and young children with incarcerated parents. In J. M. Eddy & J. Poehlmann-Tynan (Eds.), *Handbook on children with incarcerated parents: Research, policy, and practice* (pp. 85–99). Springer Nature Switzerland AG.

Ciccone, A., Dallaire, D., & Wilson L. (2010) Teacher's experiences with and expectations of children with incarcerated Parents. *Journal of Applied Developmental Psychology, 31,* 281–290.

Clifton, D. (2021). How the Trump administration's '1776 Report' warps the history or racism and slavery. *NBC News.*

Davis, A.Y. (2003). *Are prisons obsolete?* New York, NY: Seven Stories Press.

Delpit, L. (2012). *"Multiplication is for white people": Raising expectations for other people's children.* New York, NY: The New Press.

Ford, D.Y., Walters, N., Byrd, J.A., & Harris, B.N. (2018). I want to read more about me: Engaging and empowering gifted Black girls using multicultural literature and bibliotherapy. *SAGE Journalss, 42*(1), 53–57.

Handelsman, J., & Sakraney, N. (2008). *Implicit bias.* White House Office of Science and Technology Policy, pp. 1–5. https://obamawhitehouse.archives.gov/sites/default/files/microsites/ostp/bias_9-14-15_final.pdf.

Henson, A. (2021). Twitter Post. Page 1. https://twitter.com/abbie_henson/status/1382124192695414784?s=21

Khalik, A. (2017). The effectiveness of bibliotherapy as an intervention on improving aggressive behavior of fifth graders children with emotional and behavioral disorders. *International Journal of Psycho-Education Sciences, 6*(2), 30–35.

Lerner, G. (1973). *Black women in White America: A documentary history.* New York, NY: Vintage.

Lock, S. (2021). What did Rick Santorum say about Native Americans? Transcript of speech. *Newsweek.* https://www.newsweek.com/what-did-rick-santorum-say-about-native-americans-transcript-full-speech-1586628

POPS the Club. (2021). *Mission statement.* Marina Del Ray, CA. https://popsclubs.org

Turney, K. (2019). Understanding the needs of children with incarcerated parents: What educators should know. *American Federation of Teachers.* https://www.aft.org/ae/summer2019/turney

Turney, K., & Goodsell, R. (2018). Parental incarceration and children's well-being. *Future of Children, 28*(1), 147–164.

Williams, H.A. (2009). *Self-taught: African American education in slavery and freedom.* Chapel Hill: University of North Carolina Press.

5 Moving Forward
Identifying Challenges, Strengths, and Needs

The way I would change things if I was the top gun officer – I would tell everyone they don't have to be checked. They don't have to be searched. Nothing. They just got to go in, give their identification. They get their own separate rooms. They get to touch each other. There's a room and it's locked for 30 minutes. A bathroom in there, everything. They get to have a conversation. Then they knock on the door one more time to tell them they've got 30 more minutes and then when 60 minutes is up, you've got to leave. That's it.

(Tres)

Everyday parental incarceration impacts over two million minor children in the United States (Bruns & Lee, 2019; Sykes & Petit, 2014). However, parental incarceration will not impact all American children equally. In 2010, The Pew Charitable Trust found that 1 in 9 Black children have an incarcerated parent compared to 1 in 28 Hispanic children and 1 in 57 white children. Overall, 1 in every 28 children in the United States has an incarcerated parent on any given day (Pew Charitable Trusts, 2014). The average class size in a public school in the United States is about 22 students (NCES, 2021). Looking at these figures, it is very likely that a public school educator anywhere in the United States would have at least one child with an incarcerated parent in their classroom. If the educator works in a school that serves a predominately Black population, the chances of having a child with an incarcerated parent increases significantly. Therefore, even without knowing for certain that they have a child with an incarcerated parent in their class, all educators should be interested in learning more about the population and how to support them. While the previous chapters focused specifically on children of incarcerated

DOI: 10.4324/9781003202141-6

parents in schools, this chapter will look at some of the challenges and strengths of children of incarcerated parents in a larger context.

The Challenges of Supporting Children of Incarcerated Parents

Children of incarcerated parents are a unique population and no two children are identical. While incarceration impacts them all, it does it in different ways. Because of this, it is difficult to make generalized statements about children of incarcerated parents. For example, while some children know that their parent is incarcerated and why they are incarcerated, other children may have much less information. While some parents may be incarcerated within an hour of their child, other families may be separated by more than eight hours. There are some children whose caregivers may encourage a relationship with the incarcerated parent, while others do not. All of these issues (and many more) may factor into how the child experiences parental incarceration and for educators, these issues are beyond their control. However, despite this, educators can control how they support each and every child in their classroom. Being knowledgeable about parental incarceration is one way that educators can better support all of their students.

Due to the stigma that surrounds incarceration, families and children may choose to be cautious about who they disclose information to. Because children of incarcerated parents are impacted by people's biases toward incarceration and alleged criminality, they may choose not to reveal their parent's situation to anyone, including their teacher. Again, this varies. Some children may openly share while others refuse to tell anyone. I was open to answering questions about my father's whereabouts honestly if asked or if the topic came up, but as a youth I rarely shared this information unsolicited. When speaking with the youth I interviewed, none of them were keeping their parent's incarceration a total secret, but they were cautious about sharing. At first, Emmanuel was worried that his friends would make fun of him because he didn't "have a man in his life." He now says he has no problem sharing and that his friends have been supportive. Jacqueline shared with her friends, but made them promise not to tell. She indicated that she made it a "big deal" because she did not want people to spread rumors that her dad was a bad person. Despite being cautious, the youth did not always have a choice when it came to sharing their parent's incarceration with others. Jacqueline stated:

You know what's crazy? I've actually seen one of my friends in the prison seeing one of their family members I was like wait, what are you doing here? She was like oh, my god, hi, what are you doing here? We were just – we knew of each other. I was just like you look familiar and she's like I know you, we're in the same class. I'm like oh, you're what? Oh, hi. She was like I'm seeing my grandpa. I'm like I'm seeing my dad and she's like for real? I'm like, yeah. And it happened that they knew each other too.

Much like Vivett's story in chapter 4, Jacqueline was sort of forced into sharing this information with someone in her realm because the impact of incarceration in certain communities is substantial. Although my study was small, I did find that among the youth I interviewed, very few were the only ones in their social realm that had an incarcerated parent. Most of them knew someone, or multiple people their age that were also directly impacted by incarceration. This highlights the ubiquitous nature of mass incarceration in the United States, but also how it targets Black and brown communities. However, one positive that did emerge from the unfortunate prevalence of incarceration in these communities was the lessening of stigma in peer-to-peer social interactions. Tres created a deep bond with a friend who also had an incarcerated parent. He stated,

My everyday man, he going through the same thing as me. His dad was in his life. And he took a visit to see him and after that he just told me about his dad. How his dad did this stuff in prison and then we were just talking about each other's dads.

Other youth, like Amber, knew so many children with incarcerated parents that she had no qualms about sharing her experience. She stated:

Sometimes we'll have discussions [in school] about like our fathers and stuff, and I was like mine's in jail. I really don't care. I can tell people. Because most of their fathers are in jail. There's not really that many kids that have fathers in their life. Either they ran off, or they're doing time.

While the goal is to lower the number of people incarcerated and therefore the number of children experiencing parental incarceration, it may be worthwhile for future research to look that ways stigma differs depending on the prevalence of incarceration in the community. While high levels of incarceration are extremely damaging, one unexpected result in the youth I interviewed was that they were able to find a peer or peers that was currently experiencing the same thing and support one another. Having a friend to share the experience with may lessen the trauma youth experience and make them more comfortable sharing their experiences with parental incarceration in general. This revelation could factor into future discussions about protective factors and have implications for support programs.

There is no one-size-fits-all approach to children of incarcerated parents due to their varied circumstances. Adults may interact with this population regularly and never know it due to the personal nature of the topic. It is vital that adults, especially educators, do not wait for a child to self-identify as the child of an incarcerated parent before they begin implementing ways to support them. Creating a caring, responsive and equitable space is beneficial to all youth, but particularly children of incarcerated parents. Having a strong network is a vital protective factor for youth impacted by incarceration. In my study, some of the youth were creating a network of friends and associates also impacted by incarceration. However, a person does not have to be directly impacted to be a strong ally and form part of this supportive network. One of the biggest challenges to supporting children of incarcerated parents is simply knowing who they are. This is likely to remain a challenge for quite some time as there is no formal system for tracking or identifying children of incarcerated parents and families are often hesitant to share because of stigma. To remove this challenge, adult allies have to remove the condition of needing to know in order to induce action. Yes, it would be very helpful to know which child has an incarcerated parent and sometimes that will happen, but with or without that knowledge, support can start now.

Unique Universal

Ann Adalist-Estrin (2014), director of the National Research Center on Children and Families of the Incarcerated, was once said, "Children of incarcerated parents are: like all children, like some children, like no children." Eddy and Poehlmann (2019) echoed this sentiment stating:

> Like all children, the day-to-day lives of children of incarcerated parents are imbedded in family, school and community contexts. Unlike other children, however, the lives of children of incarcerated

parents are heavily influenced by a powerful "fourth" context, the criminal justice system...

(p. 6)

Children of incarcerated parents are like their peers in many ways. Like many teens, the youth I interviewed enjoyed social media, had thoughts of college and the future, and were very invested in their friendships. They were in the process of figuring out who they are and who they want to be. Many of our conversations centered around normal teenage experiences. They discussed issues such as school, love, friendships and family that seemed universal, at least in the context of American adolescence. However, their separation from their parent gave them an experience that only some children can relate to. Children of incarcerated parents are sometimes grouped with other children who have been separated from their parents such as those who have a parent who died, those who have a deployed military parent, and those who have divorced parents. In some ways, these groups of children are comparable to one another. Each group is physically separated from their parent and may experience issues such as anxiety or depression stemming from this separation. Children who are separated from their parents may require additional support from the adults in their lives, including educators. Yet, children of incarcerated parents remain a unique group. Parental incarceration presents a distinctive set of challenges and circumstances that the other groups do not have to navigate. In addition to experiencing early interactions with the criminal justice system, external reactions heavily influence the experience of children of incarcerated parents. When a child is separated from their parent due to death, deployment, or divorce, most people are sympathetic to the situation. These children can expect to receive support and in cases of deployment, the child may hear their parent referred to as a "hero." Children of incarcerated parents will most likely never hear their parent referred to in such glowing terms. In fact, older children of incarcerated parents are acutely aware that society views their parent in a negative way. Sky, illustrated her this point speaking about her father. She stated:

> Everybody just think people in prison, they just bad. Like they say like my dad is a bad guy, but he's really not. He didn't do nothing wrong. He's just himself. Sometimes when I go to a visit, I just don't feel comfortable like with everybody sitting there. Like I don't trust these people. Anything could happen. They are there

for a reason, they did something bad. I just don't like bad people. I mean, some people – some people might be in there by accident, got something switched up. But I don't know their story. So to me, all them is just bad.

Her response is complex. She knows that people view her father as "bad" because he is incarcerated, but because she knows him, she is certain he is not bad. However, this grace doesn't extend to the other men incarcerated with her father, although she does leave the possibility of wrongful conviction open. Sky both rejects and embraces the view of incarceration as indicative of a character flaw. She was able to other her father in order to make sense of her contradictory beliefs. The realization that people view their parents as "bad" can cause children of incarcerated parents to be selective about who they choose to speak to about their parent's incarceration. While this is prudent considering research about the biases toward incarcerated individuals and their families, this secrecy can also limit the amount of support and resources children of incarcerated parents can access. When people speak about children of incarcerated parents, they often speak about the shame they feel concerning their parent's incarceration. While I cannot know the feelings of every child of incarcerated parents and there are some children of incarcerated parents who may feel ashamed of their parent, I also found that some children of incarcerated parents were ashamed of a society that shuns incarcerated individuals and refused to provide them with the help they need. For example, Vanessa discussed the challenges incarcerated people faced when reentering society because of their prior incarceration. She stated:

If they [people who are incarcerated] come out into the real world with no type of help, then they're on their own and that's usually how it is. Not in my family but I've experienced from other families. They don't want their kids around that type of stuff and people need, to survive, people need companionship and other people, it don't matter who they are. People die fast from being lonely than from being sick so it's probably hard to survive in the real world without companionship or people to guide you along the way.

During our conversations, Vanessa never judged her mother or father for their substance abuse issues or incarceration. Instead, she provided insight into the ways that society and the people in it fail to support and help formerly incarcerated individuals. Her assertion that loneliness can kill you was particularly affecting considering she has been separated from her parents and siblings for many years. In the future, when people write about the shame children of incarcerated parents feel, they should also examine children of incarcerated parents' critique of external forces that assume they should be ashamed.

Educational Outcomes

In the previous chapters, I placed a tremendous amount of emphasis on how schools and educators can better support children of incarcerated parents. While this is warranted, it does not negate the fact that any traumatic life experience, including parental incarceration, can cause a child to change their behavior. Multiple studies have noted that parental incarceration is related to both externalizing (fighting, destruction of school property) and internalizing (depression, anxiety) in children depending on the circumstance (Craigie, 2011; Dallaire & Wilson, 2010; Haskins, 2015, 2016; Johnson & Easterling, 2012). Many studies also note that parental incarceration is often accompanied or preceded by other ACEs in a household (Murphey & Cooper, 2015). Children of incarcerated parents may come from homes where they have already experienced other ACEs. Because of this, it is difficult to establish a causal link between parental incarceration and adverse outcomes.

Eddy and Kjellstrand (2011) state:

> Because of multiple co-occurring risks, it is unclear if parental incarceration is a risk marker (a spurious indicator of other risks within the family), an additional risk factor over and beyond the other risks the children and their families are experiencing, or a risk mechanism (a situation that leads to additional factors such as financial strain, emotional stress, social stigma, and parenting stress)...Results from these latter studies suggest that the broader psychological risks in families (such as poverty, poor parental mental health, and poor parenting or family function) rather than specifically parental incarceration account for the subsequent behavioral problems for children whose parents have been incarcerated.
>
> (p. 553)

As I previously noted, multiple studies have shown a correlation between parental incarceration and adverse educational outcomes. In my research, many of the youth I interviewed did have some behavioral issues in school at some point. Both Amber and Vanessa previously or currently attended residential schools meant to support youth with severe behavioral issues or cognitive delays. Emmanuel recounted a period during his 4th grade year, right after his father's arrest, when his grades suffered and he had to attend summer school. However, for most of the youth I interviewed, performing poorly in school was a temporary issue. It did not define their whole educational career and they were able to get back on track. For example, Delilah shared a story about realizing she had to make a change. After years of suffering sexual abuse at the hands of her foster families and finding little support at school, she began acting aggressively. She stated:

I think the place where I forgave them when I realized – it was actually one day after school I got into a fight and I had to fight a girl or whatever. And I literally – the girl I busted her head on the toilet and everything of that sort. The girl – she was – yeah, she was talking smack don't get me wrong. She was talking smack and she deserved to get beat up. But I realize what I was thinking about was not her when I was fighting her. I was not fighting that girl because of what she did. The anger I had inside me was not for her. It was for my mom and dad. So I realize, you know, if you don't let – I looked at myself in the mirror and like I was angry everything. And I just looked myself in my mirror and I was like D – if you don't straighten up, you're going to end up hurting someone. Because, you know, yeah, people deserve to be slapped when they deserve to be slapped, but you know dang well that beat up was not for that girl – it wasn't for her. It was – you were trying to – I felt a little like when they showed the video and everything and then I – I didn't feel bad, but I felt like wrong because, you know, I wasn't thinking about that girl when I was hurting her. So it was like – I felt like D – you've got to forgive – you've got to forgive because you're going to end up hating people for no reason, you know. And so I was like – I looked at myself in the mirror and I was like you just got to do better. You got to do better if you don't want end up like them you've got to straighten up. So I started straightening up, paying attention to school, getting good grades.

Deliah did display some of the behaviors that researchers connect with children of incarcerated parents. She was getting poor grades and was quick to anger. However, it should be noted that the grief she experienced due to the separation from her parents was compounded ten-fold by what happened after. Eventually she was able to come to the realization that she wanted to improve and she took the necessary steps to do that. She was able to graduate and has plans to open her own business so she can help support her family. Delilah may have come to the decision to change her behavior sooner if she had more outside support. In the conversation about children of incarcerated parents and educational outcomes, there must be space for redemption. Many studies are a snapshot of a certain time, instead of the story of a child's journey through the educational system. Depending on the youth's circumstances, their educational outcomes may vary significantly from year to year. For example, the period immediately following a parent's incarceration can be particularly stressful and it is not uncommon for children to react to that stress in a school setting. In addition, conversations around educational outcomes for children of incarcerated parents also need to examine schools and the level of support they are providing to all students. Research has shown that schools tend to punish students of color more frequently and severely than their white counterparts. Children of incarcerated parents are disproportionately children of color and it is important to keep this in mind when discussing their educational outcomes. It may behoove researchers to investigate the educational outcomes for different subsets of students (Black, disabled, LGBTQ+, undocumented, dual language learners) in a school before attributing certain outcomes to parental incarceration instead of an unsupportive and discriminatory school culture.

Positive Trauma Responses

In the Introduction, I discussed the role I felt my father's incarceration played in my educational experience. I felt a self-induced pressure to succeed academically and being a "good" student was a central part of my identity. A lot of my people in my life viewed my desire to earn high grades as a positive. Siegel and Luther (2019) state:

> Qualitative research has also revealed that children may react to parental incarceration in constructive ways. Some children of incarcerated parents engage in coping methods that include focusing on positive avenues that they can control, such attending school or therapy; participating in athletic and theater activities or engaging in religion...These methods allowed children to adapt to parental incarceration in positive ways, leading some researchers to connect these behaviors to resilience.
>
> (p. 152)

The youth I interviewed displayed a variety of interests from athletics to paleontology and dance. All of the youth I interviewed were determined to succeed and not just for self-serving reasons. Vanessa wants to become a senator so she could help create new legislation about foster care, a system she knows well. Emmanuel wants to play professional sports so he could support his mother who sacrificed so much to care for him and his younger brother. Jacqueline is interested in becoming a detective because she believes she can "make a difference" in this position and help people. Throughout my interviews, it was evident that my collaborators had a strong desire to be of service to others, especially family and friends. Their desire to help was often related to something negative they or someone they loved experienced.

While I am an advocate for a greater focus on the strengths of children of incarcerated parents, it is important to note that just because a child seems to be responding in a positive or socially acceptable way, does not mean that they don't need support. Throughout my school career, none of my teachers spoke to me about my father's incarceration and I am not certain they even knew. Because I received good grades and was quiet in class, my teachers did not inquire about my home life. When I became an educator, I realized that often when a child is performing to a teacher's liking, meaning they are receiving sufficient grades and are not disruptive, the teacher assumes that the child is doing well overall. When a child is exhibiting concerning behavior or behavior that is disruptive to the classroom, such as low grades or frequent outbursts, the teacher becomes a detective looking for a reason for the child's perceived shortcomings and the first place they usually want to know more about is home. This is not unreasonable, but it is also not foolproof. For one, it is possible for children of incarcerated parents have internalizing behaviors. A quiet child may also indicate a withdrawn or depressed child. Two, if a child is displaying undesirable behaviors and the teacher happens to find out they have an incarcerated parent, they may incorrectly assume that the incarceration has to be the source of the problem. This assumption can lead educators to overlook other factors including their own teaching style and relationship with the child. If educators do not take the time to build relationships with their students and get to know them as much as possible, they may make assumptions that can hinder their ability to support the child.

In response to years of problem-based research, some researchers (myself included) are advocating for more strength-based research focused on children of incarcerated parents. For many researchers, one strength-based approach is a focus on the resilience of children of incarcerated parents. Shlafer et al. (2019) state, "There is also a real need for resilience-focused research-empirical work the recognizes and examines the factors associated with children and adolescents' successful adaptation despite the considerable adversities they experience in the context of parental incarceration" (p. 111). It is important to note that while resilience is considered a positive descriptor, it can be a loaded term, especially when speaking about people of color. Resilience implies the ability to endure challenging conditions and the term applies to both people of color and children of incarcerated parents. However, when a group is constantly referred to as strong or resilient they may feel the need to live up to that perception, causing them to neglect or hide the emotions attached to traumatic situations. It also may cause others to underestimate the amount of support that group needs since it appears they can endure a tremendous amount of adversity. It is important to remember that while children of incarcerated parents and children of color are resilient, they should not have to be. It is wonderful to be resilient. It would be even better if certain groups didn't have to be more resilient because they are consistently dealing with society-induced trauma and adversity. Instead of solely focusing on how to lessen the impact of the challenges, there should be an emphasis on how to prevent the challenges from existing. While examining the resiliency of children of incarcerated parents could and most likely will produce valuable data, children of incarcerated parents are amazing in ways that do not directly connect to incarceration. It is important to view them as whole people because while parental incarceration is a part of their life, it's not their whole life.

Changing the Narrative

Children of incarcerated parents are often portrayed as a vulnerable population who are susceptible to mental health problems, substance abuse issues, poor educational outcomes, problematic behavior and criminality. While I am not disputing the legitimacy of these findings – although I take issue with the link to future criminality – I do believe they present a lopsided portrait of a complex and diverse group. Because parental separation, especially due to incarceration, can be such a traumatic event, it is not unreasonable to assume it has an impact on a child. It is also reasonable to hypothesize that the impact is negative. Researchers have spent decades trying to pinpoint the detrimental effects of parental incarceration and during this time, the amount that we know about this population has increased greatly. However, this consistent focus on problems has created a one-dimensional picture of children of incarcerated parents that is overwhelmingly negative.

When studies find that teachers have lowered expectations of children with incarcerated parents because bias and stigma are present, researchers should examine how they may have contributed to certain perceptions. The creation of this negative narrative about children of incarcerated parents was no doubt unintentional, but good intentions do not negate consequences. In the future, people should show as much interest in the strengths of children of incarcerated parents as the perceived weaknesses. There is an obligation, not to gloss over or sugarcoat the experiences of children of incarcerated parents, but to provide balance to previous framing which often occurred without the input of any of the children themselves. When I asked the youth collaborators I interviewed to describe themselves, none of them said crazy, dumb, angry, or harmful. Instead, they highlighted the good in themselves. Vanessa – who survived her parent's substance abuse issues, parental incarceration, the foster care system, and numerous incidents of abuse – described herself as an "optimistic go-getter." That was who she knew she was despite several incidents when the world tried to tell her different. Allies of children of incarcerated parents should make space for them to tell us who they are instead of attempting to project a narrative onto them.

Future Research

The amount of research on children with incarcerated parents has increased substantially in the last 20 years. This is a welcome event because there was a period when the imprisoned population increased dramatically, but little attention was paid to the way this increase affected families and communities. Because of this, children of incarcerated parents were once deemed an invisible population. It was evident that some people who were imprisoned were parents, but there was not much insight or perhaps even interest into their experience. While that has changed, there are ways that children of incarcerated parents still remain invisible or rather ways in which adults hide them from view. There is a growing movement in research to be inclusive of the communities included in studies. Research holds an air of authority in American society. It is used to inform policy decisions and it also finds its way into the professional development and resources that practitioners utilize. Therefore, it is important that research is conducted and developed with community it aims to investigate. As Hollins et al. (2019) state:

> ...opening up to a broader set of inputs and embracing non-traditional partners and research methodologies has the potential

to greatly enrich the value and relevance of the stories researchers can tell. In turn, this may deepen the meaning of these stories for others and expand their implications for future actions of significance to the children of incarcerated parents. In short, if the goal of some researchers' work is to practically contribute to improving the well-being of children with incarcerated parents, researchers would benefit tremendously from the input of those who have experienced parental incarceration.

(p. 322)

As people become more aware about the experiences of children of incarcerated parents and their visibility increases, researchers have to make sure they do not hide them again. Children of incarcerated parents should also be visible in the studies conducted concerning them and the publications that feature them. This could look many ways. For example, a researcher may decide to conduct youth participatory action research (YPAR), where children of incarcerated parents act as co-investigators and are present in each step of the research process, including deciding the research question(s). It could also look like researchers including the actual words of children of incarcerated parents in their publications instead of continually paraphrasing or drawing their own implications. While this may not mirror traditional research, it is more important to value lived experience than to maintain the status quo. When appropriate, researchers could also ask children of incarcerated parents about their own experiences instead of attempting to learn about their experiences through their caregivers or teachers. In addition, instead of continually building on prior research, such as the decades-long focus on an intergenerational crime link, researchers could develop new and interesting areas of inquiry with the assistance of children with incarcerated parents. While prior research can be helpful, it can also be limiting. Researchers should attempt to free themselves from the confines of the status quo and collaborate with communities to develop studies that the community feels are important and beneficial, not just academia. If researchers really want to support children of incarcerated parents, they should consciously make sure they are present and visible in the work they are doing.

What We Can Do

One of the greatest things we can do for children of incarcerated parents is advocating for the reform or abolition of jails and prisons.

While the incarcerated population has steadily been decreasing for years, the United States still has the highest incarceration rate in the world. Simply put, the more the people who are imprisoned, the more the children without parents. Much of the trauma surrounding parental incarceration would be mitigated if we had a less punitive system that did not view long periods of incarceration as the consequence for so many things. While some people may read this and think that imprisonment is a necessary evil, it is important to note that increasing the prison population has done little to increase public safety. The rate of violent crimes has not decreased significantly over the last four decades since the prison boom (Alexander, 2010; Davis, 2003; Drucker, 2018). In fact, the United States remains one of the world's most violent developed nations. The War on Drugs has criminalized substance abuse and people imprisoned for drug-related offenses rarely get the support they need to overcome addiction. The United States also imprisons people for drugs that other countries do not and yet this has not decreased the use of recreational drugs in this country. Recently, there has been a movement to decriminalize the use of marijuana in this country that has affected laws in numerous states. Despite this, many people, particularly poor people of color, are incarcerated for marijuana-related offenses. Black people are more likely to be incarcerated for a marijuana-related offense than white people despite equal levels of use (Oleck, 2020). Significantly decreasing the prison population is a social and racial justice issue. Significantly reducing the prison population, puts more people, specifically more parents back in homes or at least back in the lives of their children. Reform or abolishment would hopefully lessen the amount of separations in the first place. Allies of children of incarcerated parents should first and foremost be proponents of criminal justice reform. However, simply releasing parents from imprisonment isn't enough. As Wakefield and Montagnet state:

> ...we wish to highlight how simply reducing incarceration may not yield large gains in child well-being. People who end up in prison are often struggling mightily-with poverty, mental illness, substance abuse, violence, and trauma-long before they come into contact with an arresting officer, judge, or correctional officer. Their children are often struggling right along with them.
>
> (2019, p. 33)

Systemic change would greatly benefit children of incarcerated parents. The effects of parental incarceration are often difficult to determine because there are so many compounding factors that affect these children' daily lives. While there are many issues that are worthy of discussion, racism and poverty are two factors that often impact the lives of children of incarcerated parents. Children of incarcerated parents are often children of color and children of color, specifically Black children, are more likely to live in poverty than their white counterparts. In 2019, the overall poverty rate was 10.5%. For Black people, the poverty rate was 18.8%, the lowest rate it has ever been since poverty estimates began in 1959. The poverty rate for white people in 2019 was 7.3% (Creamer, 2020). Even when the Black poverty rate is historically low, it is still more than double that of the white poverty rate. While not all Black people live in poverty, a disproportionate amount do and living in poverty has been shown to have several detrimental effects on a person's mental and physical health. Poverty is a racial justice issue. A report from the Anti-Poverty Network of New Jersey (2017) found that racism is the cause of the high poverty rates in communities of color. The report (2017) states:

> Inherent structural racism operates as a perpetuating force and serves as a resistance to change in the historic distribution of wealth. This distribution has demonstrably advantaged White families, sometimes through the exploitation of Black and Brown labor and sometimes through unequal access to economic opportunity. These historical realities have been generated by intentional and unintentional decisions, programs and policies – some malignant, some ignorant, some merely misguided…Unfortunately, the evils wrought by these immoral, unjust or ill-informed policies have over time become deeply, even invisibly embedded in today's culture and institutions. The resulting racial and ethnic disparities have become a self-perpetuating status quo. They have disappeared into "the way things are," even as they continue to unfairly limit, burden and even destroy the lives of millions of families and individuals. This historic reality does not require intentional prejudice to be a driving force in the present day. It does not require any action at all. Maintenance of the status quo, when that status quo arises from a racist history, systematizes racism in perpetuity.
>
> (p. 3)

Because a Black child's chance of having an incarcerated parent is six times higher than a white child and Black children are twice as likely to live in poverty than their white counterparts, children of incarcerated parents are more likely to be compounded by the effects of parental incarceration, racism, and poverty. As Bruns and Lee (2019) write:

> Because of residential segregation and other racialized social processes, families of color are more likely to live in under-sourced neighborhoods, which restricts children of color's access to both institutions and individuals that could opportunities for success, provide support, and help mitigate the harmful impact of incarceration in children's lives.

(p. 41)

Racism and racist policies cause people of color to be incarcerated at higher rates which means more children of color are growing up separated from their parents and impacted by the trauma of parental incarceration. Once this occurs, racist social processes confine them to spaces where they have less access to support and protective factors. The cycle is damaging. Big picture, one of the most important actions a person can take to support children of incarcerated parents is to engage in anti-racist work. Anti-racist work fights against unequitable outcomes in the criminal justice system and therefore it would decrease the amount of parents of color separated from their children. Anti-racist work also fights against the "racialized social processes" Bruns and Lee (2019) mentioned, meaning that it advocates for equitable resources and funding for communities of color. This would likely increase the educational outcomes and number of supportive resources available for children of incarcerated parents. While some may not consider it as such, work being done to support children of incarcerated parents should be considered anti-racist work because for a large portion of children with incarcerated parents, the impact of parental incarceration cannot be detached from the impact of racism in America.

Conclusion

Children of incarcerated parents face a number of challenges; however, many of these challenges are increased or at times even created by external factors. While it is important to understand how parental incarceration impacts a child, it is also important to fight against the systems and policies that created so many children of incarcerated parents in the first place. Finding ways to support children who are currently or who have previously experienced parental incarceration is very important, but the goal should be to lessen the number of children who ever experience parental incarceration. While this may sound like an issue that is out of our control, personal choice is not the only factor that determines if a person will be incarcerated. Advocates for children of incarcerated parents should also be proponents of criminal justice reform and staunch anti-racists. The staggering number of children impacted by parental incarceration is not the result of millions of individual choices; it is the result of generations of racist policies and the criminalization of poverty. This understanding should provide the foundation for research, policy, and practice moving forward. Without this understanding, our response will be short-sighted and inadequate. Without this understanding, our focus will always be on treating the symptom rather than the disease of mass incarceration in America.

References

Alexander, M. (2010). *The new Jim Crow: Mass incarceration in the age of colorblindness.* New York, NY: The New Press.

Ann Adalist-Estrin. National Resource Center on Children and Families of the Incarcerated. (2014). Fact Sheet. *Rutgers University.*

Anti-Poverty Network of New Jersey. (2017). The Uncomfortable Truth: Racism, poverty and injustice in New Jersey.

Bruns, A., & Lee, H. (2019). Racial/ethnic disparities In J.M. Eddy & J. Poehlmann-Tynan (Eds.), *Handbook on children with incarcerated parents: Research, policy and practice* (pp. 37–52). Switzerland: Springer Nature.

Craigie, T.A.L. (2011). The effect of parental incarceration on early childhood behavioral problems: A racial comparison. *Journal of Ethnicity in Criminal Justice, 9*(3), 179–199.

Creamer, J. (2020). Inequalities persist despite decline in poverty for all major race and Hispanic origin groups. *United States Census Bureau.*

Dallaire, D.H., & Wilson, L.C. (2010). The relation of exposure to parental criminal activity, arrest, and sentencing to children's maladjustment. *Journal of Child and Family Studies, 19*(4), 404–418.

Davis, A.Y. (2003). *Are prisons obsolete?* New York, NY: Seven Stories Press.

Drucker, E. (2018). *Decarcerating America: From mass punishment to public health.* New York, NY: The New Press.

Eddy, J. & Kjellstrand J. (2011). Mediators of the effect of parental incarceration on adolescent externalizing behaviors. *Journal of Community Psychology, 39*(5), 551–565.

Eddy, J.M., & Poehlmann-Tynan, J. (2019). Interdisciplinary perspectives on research and interventions with children of incarcerated parents. In J.M. Eddy & J. Poehlmann-Tynan (Eds.), *Handbook on children with incarcerated parents: Research, policy and practice* (pp. 3–10). Switzerland: Springer Nature.

Haskins, A.R. (2015). Parental Incarceration and child-reported behavioral functioning at 9. *Social Science Research, 52*(7), 18–33.

Haskins, A.R. (2016). Beyond boys' bad behavior: Parental incarceration and cognitive development in middle school. *Social Forces, 95*(2), 861–892.

Hollins, W.Q., Underwood, E., & Krupat, T. (2019). About us, for us, with us: Collaboration as the key to progress in research, practice and policy. In J.M. Eddy & J. Poehlmann-Tynan (Eds.), *Handbook on children with incarcerated parents: Research, policy and practice* (pp. 311–328). Switzerland: Springer Nature.

Johnson, E.I., & Easterling, B. (2012). Understanding unique effects of parental incarceration on children: Challenges, progress, and recommendations. *Journal of Marriage and Family, 74*(2), 342–356.

Murphey, D., & Cooper, P.M. (2015). Parents behind bars: What happens to their children? *Child Trends,* 1–20.

National Center for Education Statistics. (2021). Schools and Staffing Survey. *Institute of Education Sciences.*

Oleck, J. (2020). With 40,000 Americans incarcerated for marijuana offenses, the cannabis industry needs to step up, activist said this week. *Forbes.*

Shlafer, R.J., Davis, L., & Dallaire, D.H. (2019). Parental incarceration during middle childhood and adolescence. In J.M. Eddy & J. Poehlmann-Tynan (Eds.), *Handbook on children with incarcerated parents: Research, policy and practice* (pp. 101–116). Switzerland: Springer Nature.

Siegel, J.A., & Luther, K. (2019). Qualitative research on children of incarcerated parents: Findings, challenges, and future directions. In J.M. Eddy & J. Poehlmann-Tynan (Eds.), *Handbook on children with incarcerated parents: Research, policy and practice* (pp. 149–163). Switzerland: Springer Nature.

Sykes, B.L., & Petit, B. (2014). Mass incarceration, family complexity, and the reproduction of childhood disadvantage. *The ANNALS of the American Academy of Political and Social Science, 654*(1), 127–149.

The Pew Charitable Trusts. (2010). *Collateral costs: Incarcerations effect on economic mobility.* Washington, DC: The Pew Charitable Trusts.

Wakefield, S., & Montagnet, C. (2019). Parental criminal justice involvement. In J.M. Eddy & J. Poehlmann-Tynan (Eds.), *Handbook on children with incarcerated parents: Research, policy and practice* (pp. 25–35).Switzerland: Springer Nature.

Index

For Product Safety Concerns and Information please contact our EU
representative GPSR@taylorandfrancis.com
Taylor & Francis Verlag GmbH, Kaufingerstraße 24, 80331 München, Germany